CONSUMER REPORTS

AUTO
INSURANCE
HANDBOOK

AUTO INSURANCE HANDBOOK

—

Tobie Stanger
Bill Hartford

and the Editors of
Consumer Reports Books

CONSUMER REPORTS BOOKS

A Division of Consumers Union

Yonkers, New York

Special thanks to
Greg Daugherty and Alex Markovich
for their reviews of the contents of this book,
and our appreciation to Janet Bamford
for the use of some of her material
from *The Consumer Reports Money Book.*

Certain portions of chapters 1 and 5 have been
taken from "Automobile Insurance," by Janet Bamford,
pages 279–300 of *The Consumer Reports Money Book,*
copyright © 1992 by Consumers Union of United States.

Library of Congress Cataloging-in-Publication Data

Stanger, Tobie.
    Consumer reports auto insurance handbook / Tobie Stanger, Bill
Hartford, and the editors of Consumer Reports Books.
        p.   cm.
    Includes index.
    ISBN 0-89043-670-3
    1. Insurance, Automobile—United States.   2. Consumer education—
United States.   I. Hartford, Bill, 1938– .   II. Consumer Reports
Books.   III. Title.   IV. Title: Auto insurance handbook.
HG9979.3.S83   1993
368'.092'0973—dc20

93-26450
CIP

Design and illustrations by GDS/Jeffrey L. Ward
First printing, November 1993
Manufactured in the United States of America
This book is printed on recycled paper. ✪

To Jim and Julia, with love

—Tobie Stanger

To Shari, my constant passenger—
with the best extra pair of eyes a driver could have

—Bill Hartford

Contents

—

Introduction

—

For all the money consumers spend on auto insurance, they rarely use any of their coverage. The average American household spent $8,900 to insure its cars between 1981 and 1991 but filed just one claim, typically for about $600.

It's no wonder that auto insurance just doesn't seem worth the expense to most consumers. Many people also don't understand why they're charged so much, or why they end up in an assigned-risk pool when they've had only one accident or a few moving violations.

This book is intended to address and help alleviate this consumer frustration. In the pages that follow, we hope to unravel the complications of the auto insurance system. Among the topics covered are how rates are set, what impact state laws have on insurance premiums, why different insurers charge different amounts for the same coverage, and why they charge some drivers so much more than others. We'll examine which legis-

lative initiatives have worked to control costs and which have failed.

Most of this book, however, is devoted to offering practical advice to consumers who want to know how to get the best coverage and how to use it wisely when they do. Consumers have more control over the costs of their coverage than they may realize, so we explain the basic coverages and how drivers can choose the best mix for their needs.

We've also examined which coverages are essential and which deductibles and discounts can lower the cost of your premium. You will also find advice on avoiding certain pitfalls, such as sales pitches for auto rental insurance or deals from a financially shaky insurer.

Service can be just as important a factor as price in auto insurance shopping. In the pages that follow, we've explained which aspects of service are most important to consumers and which insurers serve their customers best. Throughout the book, we refer to *Consumer Reports* magazine's unique Ratings of 49 auto insurance companies. The Ratings, compiled from a 1991 Annual Questionnaire to readers, were first published in the magazine in August 1992. The nearly 257,000 readers who answered the auto insurance questions in the survey included some 63,000 consumers who had filed claims in the previous three years— enough to give at least 200 claim experiences for each of the companies rated (and many more for the biggest companies). Overall, more than 40 percent of readers who filed claims within that three-year period were less than completely satisfied with their auto insurers.

We can't say that the Ratings reflect the general public's experience with auto insurance; these are simply the opinions of the readers of *Consumer Reports*. They are, however, the most comprehensive service ratings of auto insurers available to consumers. Similarly, ser-

vice may have changed among some of the rated companies since the survey. But because these Ratings closely resemble those published back in 1984 and 1988, we feel they accurately portray service today, particularly among the top-rated companies.

Getting the best value in auto insurance also means driving safely and understanding how to protect your car against vandalism and theft. Part II of this book presents a detailed review of what it means to own and drive a car today—from observing good driving habits to reporting an accident. One important section is on defensive driving techniques that can help consumers avoid the moving violations and accidents that increase their insurance costs. Other chapters include advice and tips on driving at night or in bad weather, security devices that offer the most protection, and driving tips for older people.

PART ONE

HOW TO SHOP
FOR
AUTO INSURANCE

—

1

The Policy: Coverages and Options
—

Automobile insurance protects you from the cost of damage to your car and to yourself. It also protects you against the claims of those who have sustained damage from, or have been injured by, your vehicle.

In 1991 alone, there were some 31.3 million auto accidents in the United States—one for every five licensed drivers. According to the National Safety Council, the cost of those accidents was substantial: 43,500 deaths, nearly 5.3 million injuries, and an economic cost (from property damage, medical costs, lost productivity, the cost of emergency services, legal and court costs, public assistance programs, and insurance administration expenses) estimated at an astounding $93.8 billion.

To help protect the public from that burden, auto insurance is the law in most states. Registered car owners in 41 states and the District of Columbia must have certain minimum levels of auto liability insurance. In states without compulsory auto insurance laws, drivers who don't carry insurance must prove, either before or after an accident, that they can pay the required minimum coverage in their state. Obviously, it's more convenient to buy insurance coverage on a regular basis than to satisfy officials about your current financial situation.

THE POLICY: STANDARD INSURANCE PROTECTION

An auto insurance policy is a package of several types of coverage. Some coverage is mandatory and some is optional, depending on the laws of your state. Each coverage carries its own price, or *premium*; the sum of these premiums is the total amount you pay for your policy. You can raise or lower the price tag by increasing or decreasing the amount of these coverages (see chapter 4).

Keep in mind, however, that the main purpose of any type of insurance is to protect you against serious accidents, not the small nicks and dents of parking-lot collisions. Coverage that reimburses you for every dime may cost much more than it's worth. Besides, most drivers can afford to pay out of pocket for small mishaps—a broken window, a dented bumper—without using their insurance.

A good auto insurance policy is also broad in its coverage. It should protect you in many different situations. Very specific coverage—such as towing insurance—usually isn't worth the money. So, at every step of the insurance-shopping process, think about what you really need and don't consider the unimportant items.

Most standard auto insurance policies carry the following coverages.

Bodily Injury Liability

In most states, the only type of coverage you must carry is liability—which is insurance that protects others against damage you may cause by your own driving. This coverage pays the injured party's bills and also your legal costs if you are sued. It is the most necessary coverage and, in many states, the most expensive. Liability insurance has two components: bodily injury and property damage.

Bodily injury liability pays for losses resulting from death or injury in an accident in which you were the one at fault. The people you injure can collect against this coverage to pay their medical bills and lost wages, and to compensate for their pain and suffering.

All insurance has limits, though, which means that there is a maximum amount the insurer will pay per accident or per person. Depending on the company, you can buy bodily injury liability coverage with either a multiple ("split") limit or a single limit. *Split-limit policies* pay a certain amount to each person injured in an accident. The total amount paid out, however, is subject to a maximum for each accident. If the policy pays a maximum of $100,000 per person and $300,000 per accident, and one person suffered damages of $200,000, the policy would pay only $100,000 to that individual. And if four people suffered injury in a single accident, the policy would pay up to $300,000 for total damages.

A *single-limit policy* pays one amount per accident, regardless of how many individuals are involved. This policy is slightly more expensive than the equivalent amount of split-limit coverage because it potentially provides more benefits per person. If the driver carried $300,000 of single-limit coverage and only one person was injured, that individual could collect up to $300,000.

States that mandate automobile insurance specify minimum levels of liability coverage. These minimums are typically expressed in a form of industry shorthand: For example, 25/50/10 indicates that an insurer will pay a maximum of $25,000 to each person injured in an accident, a maximum of $50,000 for everyone injured, and $10,000 to cover all property damage caused by the accident (see chart on pages 8–9).

For most drivers, however, the required minimum levels of liability insurance are not enough. If a judgment entered against you exceeds the limit your insurance company will pay, you may have to pay the remainder out of your own personal assets. This may mean dipping into your savings, liquidating investments, or even selling property to pay the damage award. These days, automobile damage awards can be large, although the much-publicized million-dollar judgments are frequently reduced on appeal or in posttrial settlements.

Property Damage Liability

Just as you are responsible for paying expenses when your driving causes bodily injuries or death, you probably will be liable if you cause damage to property.

The most common type of property damage in an auto accident involves another automobile, but damage to buildings, telephone poles, and fences isn't unusual.

As with bodily injury liability coverage, most states require that you carry a certain level of property damage insurance, ranging anywhere from $5,000 to $25,000. The most common minimum—required by 30 states—is $10,000 of coverage. But again, experts advise that you carry at least $25,000 to $50,000; an accident that damages several cars, or even one expensive car, can easily cost more than $10,000.

Generally, increasing your liability coverage to a more adequate level doesn't add much to your premium and may be worth the additional expense. Upgrading a basic 25/50/10 policy to 100/300/25 will cost the average driver about $55 annually, according to State Farm, one of the largest auto insurers in the country.

A more cost-effective strategy is to buy *umbrella* coverage. As the name suggests, the umbrella is an all-encompassing policy; it covers liability costs that exceed the dollar limits on both your auto and homeowner's policies. An umbrella policy may also cover you in special situations, such as being sued for libel, slander, mental anguish, humiliation, or false arrest. Most insurers require you to have both auto and homeowner's (or renter's) policies with them to qualify for an umbrella policy. A $1 million umbrella policy costs about $200 a year. You also may have to buy a certain amount of auto liability coverage—perhaps 100/300/50—before you're eligible for umbrella coverage.

What should you do, however, if you have a low-paying job, rent your apartment, and don't own any substantial assets other than your car? In that case, you may prefer to pay for insurance within your state's minimum liability limits. Such coverage pays the other party following an accident, but not you. Why buy coverage to protect assets you don't have?

COMPULSORY LIMITS FOR AUTOMOBILE LIABILITY INSURANCE

Listed below are the minimum state requirements for automobile liability insurance. The first figure refers to the maximum that the coverage would pay for each person injured in an accident; the second figure refers to the maximum the coverage would pay per accident. In Arkansas, for example, the minimum coverage would pay up to $50,000 per accident but no more than $25,000 per person injured in that accident. The third figure refers to the maximum the coverage would pay for property damage in a single accident. Motorists can—and are usually advised to—buy liability insurance at higher limits than state mandates.

STATE	PERSONAL INJURY LIMIT	PER-ACCIDENT LIMIT	PROPERTY DAMAGE LIMIT
Alabama	$20,000	$40,000	$10,000
Alaska	50,000	100,000	25,000
Arizona	15,000	30,000	10,000
Arkansas	25,000	50,000	15,000
California	15,000	30,000	5,000
Colorado	25,000	50,000	15,000
Connecticut	20,000	40,000	10,000
Delaware	15,000	30,000	10,000
District of Columbia	25,000	50,000	10,000
Florida	10,000	20,000	10,000
Georgia	15,000	30,000	10,000
Hawaii	15,000	35,000	10,000
Idaho	25,000	50,000	15,000
Illinois	20,000	40,000	15,000
Indiana	25,000	50,000	10,000
Iowa	20,000	40,000	15,000
Kansas	25,000	50,000	10,000
Kentucky	25,000	50,000	10,000
Louisiana	10,000	20,000	10,000
Maine	20,000	40,000	10,000
Maryland	20,000	40,000	10,000
Massachusetts	20,000	40,000	5,000
Michigan	20,000	40,000	10,000
Minnesota	30,000	60,000	10,000
Mississippi	10,000	20,000	5,000
Missouri	25,000	50,000	10,000
Montana	25,000	50,000	5,000
Nebraska	25,000	50,000	25,000
Nevada	15,000	30,000	10,000

STATE	PERSONAL INJURY LIMIT	PER-ACCIDENT LIMIT	PROPERTY DAMAGE LIMIT
New Hampshire	$25,000	$50,000	$25,000
New Jersey	15,000	30,000	5,000
New Mexico	25,000	50,000	10,000
New York	10,000*	20,000*	5,000
North Carolina	25,000	50,000	10,000
North Dakota	25,000	50,000	25,000
Ohio	12,500	25,000	7,500
Oklahoma	10,000	20,000	10,000
Oregon	25,000	50,000	10,000
Pennsylvania	15,000	30,000	5,000
Rhode Island	25,000	50,000	25,000
South Carolina	15,000	30,000	5,000
South Dakota	25,000	50,000	25,000
Tennessee	20,000	50,000	10,000
Texas	20,000	40,000	15,000
Utah	20,000	40,000	10,000
Vermont	20,000	40,000	10,000
Virginia	25,000	50,000	20,000
Washington	25,000	50,000	10,000
West Virginia	20,000	40,000	10,000
Wisconsin	25,000	50,000	10,000
Wyoming	25,000	50,000	20,000

*$50,000 and $100,000 if injury results in death
Sources: Insurance Information Institute and American Insurance Association

Uninsured or Underinsured Motorist Protection

An alarming number of people drive around without automobile insurance. If you are hit by one of them and you are not sufficiently insured, you are in trouble. You can, of course, try to recover damages from the driver's personal assets, but chances are that a driver who doesn't have insurance probably doesn't have much in the way of assets either.

To guard against such a situation, you can buy *uninsured* motorist coverage. (It is even required in 21 states.) With this insurance, you look to your own policy to insure what's not covered by the other motorist's policy. Most uninsured motorist policies cover only bodily injuries; some pay for damage to your car as well. This protection also covers you if you are in an accident with a hit-and-run driver.

States that do require uninsured motorist coverage typically set minimums of around $25,000 per person and $50,000 per accident. That coverage, offered through State Farm's subsidiaries, for example, would cost the average driver $10 a year. However, it's a good idea to buy more coverage, and many people buy it in amounts as high as their bodily injury liability coverage. After all, this is the coverage that protects you, not the other driver. Raising this coverage from $25/$50 to $100/$300 costs $7 a year more, on average.

You cannot buy higher limits for uninsured motorist protection than the bodily injury limits you have chosen.

There are exceptions to the coverage: Uninsured motorist protection won't pay if you or a member of your family owns the car that hit you and it is not insured, or if the car is a government-owned vehicle. Nor will it cover you if you are struck by a vehicle designed for use off public roads (tractor, snowmobile, or an all-terrain vehicle) while that vehicle is operating off public roads.

If you live in a state without good no-fault laws (see box on page 60), it's wise to buy this coverage. (Unlike traditional tort liability insurance, no-fault coverage you buy pays for your injuries in an accident regardless of who is at fault.) As premiums rise, more and more drivers are neglecting to carry insurance or are failing to renew a policy they purchased earlier solely to satisfy registration requirements. Today there is a greater chance that your car may be hit by a driver without the coverage to pay for your injuries.

Similarly, rising medical costs have in-

creased the need for a related coverage—protection against *underinsured* drivers. (Such coverage is mandatory in only a few states.) If you are injured by someone with only minimum liability coverage and your damages exceed the limits of the driver's policy, your underinsured motorist coverage will begin to pay where the other coverage ends.

Personal-Injury Protection (PIP)

In states with no-fault laws, you are required to buy personal-injury protection (PIP), which pays for your medical costs—and other accident-related expenses—regardless of who was at fault.

PIP covers not only your medical bills but the income lost if you are unable to work. It will also guarantee replacement services if you are unable to perform routine tasks, such as child care. It also may pay some funeral expenses. Drivers in no-fault states can buy up to $50,000 of PIP coverage, but most buy only $10,000.

If your state's no-fault rules allow policyholders to coordinate benefits with their health insurance policies, you may save on PIP premiums. By electing to make your health insurance *primary*—that is, by seeking reimbursements for accident-related medical expenses from your health insurer before applying to your auto insurer—you could reduce your premium for personal-injury protection by as much as 40 percent.

Medical Payments Insurance

In states without no-fault laws, drivers can cover their own injuries through medical payments insurance. An optional coverage, this type of insurance will pay regardless of who was at fault. Medical payments insurance covers family members and guests who happen to be riding in the policyholder's car. You and your family are also covered if you're hit by a car while walking or riding a bicycle, or if you're injured while riding in someone else's car (typically, that driver's coverage will reimburse you up to the limits of his or her policy; after that, your own coverage takes over). If a driver or passenger is killed, this insurance often pays for funeral expenses. The insurance covers each person injured; $10,000 worth of medical payments coverage will pay $10,000 for each person injured.

Again, many people with good health insurance policies can forgo auto medical payments insurance, since injuries sustained in an accident may well be covered under standard medical and hospital insurance. But a small amount of additional coverage may make sense. For one thing, health insurance usually doesn't pay a funeral benefit. (On the other hand, a good life insurance policy will cover this contingency.) Medical payments coverage also will compensate nonfamily members who may be injured while riding in your car. Their medical bills will then be paid immediately by your carrier. Without such a plan, injured passengers would have to sue to collect against your liability coverage.

Collision Insurance

This type of protection pays for damage to your car if it is in a collision or if it rolls over, regardless of who was responsible for the accident. If you are not at fault, your insurer may pay you for damages and then try to get reimbursed from the other driver or from the driver's insurance company.

Collision coverage is always limited by a deductible, which is the amount you pay out of pocket after an accident, before the coverage begins. Deductibles of $100 to $250 are the most common, but they can be as high as $2,000.

If you are considering the purchase of collision insurance, ask yourself whether or not you need it and, if so, what kind of deductible makes sense to you. For example, if you have a new or expensive car, you should have collision insurance; in fact, if you have an auto loan outstanding, the lender probably will insist that you carry collision coverage until the loan is repaid. It is also usually worthwhile to carry collision coverage for cars less than three years old. If a car is between three and seven years old, your decision will depend on how much risk you are willing to assume. Generally, you don't need collision coverage for cars older than seven years.

It makes sense to drop collision coverage entirely on an older car with a low resale value, because the resale, or "book," value of a car also represents the maximum an insurer will pay you for the car if it is totaled in an accident. Most cars made in the United States depreciate rapidly. After five years, a domestic car is typically worth only about 30 percent of what it cost originally. (Some foreign cars depreciate less rapidly; a few even appreciate in value.) So the amount you would be reimbursed by your insurer could be quite small, especially when you compare it to the premiums you have to pay for the insurance.

If you do decide that collision coverage is warranted, you can save on the insurance premium by taking a higher deductible. For example, you can save from 15 to 30 percent on your premium if you take a $500 deductible instead of a $250 deductible. Because it's unlikely that you would file a collision claim every year, you'll probably save over the long run with a higher deductible.

These savings can be significant, especially in localities with high insurance rates. Depending on where you live, a collision premium can account for as much as a third of the total cost of auto insurance.

Comprehensive Insurance

Comprehensive insurance is the companion to collision coverage. While collision covers accident-related damage to your car, comprehensive covers just about everything else that might befall an automobile. If the car is stolen or vandalized, comprehensive coverage takes care of your loss. If your car is hit by falling objects, if it catches fire, if there is glass breakage, or if it is damaged in a flood, you turn to comprehensive coverage for reimbursement. If you hit a deer on a stormy night, comprehensive insurance, not collision, covers the damage to your car.

Comprehensive does not cover mechanical breakdown of the car, however, or normal wear and tear. If your fan belt breaks or there's a leak in the radiator, it's up to you to pay for repairs. Comprehensive insurance also doesn't usually cover losses related to accessories—such as tape decks, radios, CBs, or car telephones—unless they are permanently installed in the car.

Some comprehensive policies will cover the loss of any personal property in the car if the loss occurs because of fire, lightning, or sometimes theft. Comprehensive insurance, however, is primarily designed to cover the car itself, not what's in it. If you do lose belongings that were inside your car, a homeowner's or renter's policy may cover such losses. Comprehensive insurance also may cover the cost of a rental car (within certain monetary limits and for a limited period of time) if your own car is stolen. As with collision insurance, think twice about how much, if any, comprehensive coverage you need on an older car. The most an insurer will pay is the current resale, or market, value.

The price of comprehensive insurance varies with the kind of car you own and where you live. Luxury and sports cars are stolen most frequently; station wagons are stolen the least. And because of the higher incidence of car theft in cities, comprehensive coverage is more expensive in urban areas than in suburban and rural parts of the country.

Each comprehensive policy is sold with a deductible, which ranges from

$50 to $500. The higher the deductible, the lower the insurance bill, so consumers should choose the highest deductible they can afford.

Optional Policy Coverages
Rental Reimbursement Insurance. If you're covered by rental reimbursement insurance, you'll be paid for some or all car rental expenses while your car is out of commission, or until you purchase a new car. Policies and costs vary, but there are usually strict limits to this coverage. One basic policy, for example, pays the average driver up to $16 a day, to a maximum of $400, for rental of a car. In addition, the policy pays for taxi fares or other commercial transportation if you're more than 50 miles from home, as well as the collision and comprehensive deductibles in the event you have an accident in the rental car. The cost of this coverage is about $25 a year.

Towing and Labor Insurance. Towing and labor coverage pays for the cost of having your car towed in the event of an accident or breakdown. Some companies pay a set amount for this service—perhaps $25—whereas others pay what's customary and reasonable in the area where the car is towed. Only labor actually performed at the scene of the breakdown is covered. This coverage is inexpensive (about $4 a year), but you can do without it if you belong to an auto club that provides towing services with membership.

Auto Death Indemnity. This option pays a limited amount if a policyholder dies in an accident or from injuries sustained in an accident. (The coverage doesn't require fault to be established.) Some insurers include coverage for dismemberment, paying on a sliding scale that depends on the severity of the injury. If you live in a no-fault state, your personal-injury protection (PIP) already covers this contingency. If you don't, a good life insurance policy is probably a better buy.

Auto Disability Income. This optional coverage pays a weekly stipend to a policyholder who is disabled as a result of an auto accident. Depending on the policy, you may be entitled to this income even if you have received a bodily injury payment and disability income from your employer. Again, no-fault insurance or a good disability policy already includes this coverage.

HOW TO READ A POLICY

Contrary to popular belief, you don't have to be a genius to understand your auto insurance policy. True, a policy is not fun reading, but knowing what's covered and what's not can save you from shock and disappointment later when you file a claim.

Some states have come to the aid of consumers by mandating easy-to-read auto insurance policies. Even in those states, however, an agent or customer service representative may need to explain certain words or phrases to policyholders. Don't hesitate to ask if you don't understand something in your policy. It is a legal contract, and you have the right to know your (and your insurer's) rights and obligations.

The following description and explanation of items found in a standard auto insurance policy may help you understand the extent of your coverages.

The Declarations Page

Generally the first page of any policy, the declarations page states the basics: which cars are covered, names of all drivers, types of insurance selected, and the insurance limits and costs. Many insurers also itemize here any included surcharges or discounts.

It's a good idea to check the declarations page to ensure that the proper car has been assigned to the proper driver. This can have an impact on the overall premium. Make sure, too, that other information, such as annual mileage and the vehicle identification number (VIN), is accurate for each vehicle. This, too, can affect your premium. The VIN, for example, indicates whether your insured car has built-in air bags, which makes you automatically eligible for insurance discounts in some states.

The most crucial information in determining your premiums is your car's ratings classification. That classification is usually expressed as a multidigit number. Each digit or pair of digits stands for some category: driver's age group or gen-

der, the uses of the vehicle, etc. Some insurers include a list identifying what each digit means, so you can double-check that the information about you and your cars is accurate. If you don't understand the codes, ask an agent or customer service representative to explain them to you.

The Insuring Agreement

The bulk of the policy consists of an agreement outlining the who, what, where, when, and other details for each type of coverage you've purchased. The beginning of the agreement usually defines terms.

Who. The agreement states in detail who's covered: the insured and relatives, passengers, and people given permission to drive the car. A relative may be defined as someone who not only is related to the insured drivers listed on the declarations page, but is also a full-time resident of the policyholder's household.

What. Besides covering any car named in the policy, the insurance may cover an auto you use temporarily because the insured car was stolen, in the shop, or otherwise unusable. It may also cover rented trailers.

Where. Most policies cover vehicles driven in the United States, its territories, and Canada. The agreement explains what the insurer's responsibilities are if you have an accident in another state.

When. If you've insured your car for commuting or pleasure driving, you generally won't be covered should you use the car for business purposes or as a "livery" vehicle.

How long. The agreement probably will outline how long the company will continue paying for certain damages. Medical payments coverage, for example, may only pay for expenses incurred within three years of a reported accident.

How much. The agreement's *limit of liability* explains just how much of each coverage it will pay, and whether having other insurance—such as health coverage—will affect the payment.

Endorsements

The forms that outline additions in coverage are attached to the main policy and are called endorsements. For example, the insurer may have special coverages for customized vans, trailers, and campers. Or it may offer special protection for electronic equipment that is not covered in the main policy. If your policy includes endorsements, the identifying numbers for each one should be noted on the declarations page. Make sure you're being charged only for the proper coverage.

Think carefully, however, before buying such additions to your policy. They usually provide very narrow coverages, which probably makes them bad deals. It may be cheaper in the long run to cover the costs of any of these potential damages out of pocket.

Exclusions

Pay particular attention to the exclusions in each section. In the comprehensive portion of the policy, for example, coverage may specifically exclude motorcycles and any other "motorized vehicle having fewer than four wheels." Comprehensive coverage also may not

WHO WAS DRIVING THE CAR?

Who is covered, and when, can become a major issue when you have to file an auto insurance claim. Despite specific wording in the agreement, policies lend themselves to varied interpretations depending on the jurisdiction where you live.

For example, your policy probably states that it doesn't cover anyone whom you would not normally allow to drive your car. That stipulation can lead to tricky situations. Suppose your daughter (who is covered in the policy) allows a friend to drive your car, and the friend has an accident. Insurers in some states could maintain that you, the policyholder, didn't give permission to the friend to drive the car, so the friend is not covered for any injuries.

But the friend may have been driving your daughter home because she was intoxicated or sick. In many states, you could effectively argue that, had you been asked, you would have given the friend permission to drive. For this reason, the friend probably would be considered covered by your policy.

include damage to sound systems that haven't been built into the car, as well as damage to mobile phones, audio- and videocassette recorders and tapes, computers, and CB radios. Generally, your car is covered if it suffers damage during "riot or civil commotion" but not if it's damaged in "war or insurrection."

Conditions and Other Provisions

Your responsibilities and rights are outlined in the portion of the policy dealing with conditions. For example, you must report an accident promptly and agree to cooperate fully with any investigations that result. Another condition gives you the right to cancel a policy at any time, although the company can only cancel under certain circumstances.

This section of the policy also indicates when you're allowed to sue the insurer and what steps the insurer can take when it wants to make a change in the coverage. If, for example, you leave the insurer or the insurer drops you, it still has an obligation to follow up and resolve any of your outstanding claims.

2

How Auto Insurance Is Priced

—

A *Pontiac Firebird TransAm* costs about $21,000 to buy, but if you are a young man in Detroit, you could spend more than $9,000 a year just to insure it. In Philadelphia, a married couple with a teenage son could spend more than $7,500 a year to insure both a *Honda Accord* and a *Toyota Corolla*. And a retired couple driving a nine-year-old *Oldsmobile Delta 88* in San Francisco could pay more than $1,300 a year, though the car itself is worth no more than $3,000.

No wonder the price of auto insurance ranks so high on many consumers' gripe lists. To many people, the price of car insurance seems not just unreasonable but completely inexplicable. Yet, in most states, car owners are required to buy insurance.

Like any other product, however, auto insurance has certain pricing principles behind it. The more you understand them, the better you may be able to control your own insurance costs.

SETTING THE RATES: THE ACTUARIAL FACTORS

In the pricing of most goods and services, manufacturers add up the expected costs of raw materials and overhead, then determine a price that they expect will make them a fair profit. They then take their goods to the marketplace to find out, through competition, whether the price and the product will attract buyers.

The "raw materials" of the insurance business are, in essence, the costs of paying the claims of policyholders. However, insurers can't know in advance how much those claims—also called losses—will cost them. As a result, much of insurance pricing is a fine-tuned prediction: Insurers use statistics and experience from the past to estimate their future costs. In insurance parlance, a company's past history of paying claims is its *loss experience*.

That loss experience can be different for every type, or line, of insurance that a company sells. And the loss experience can differ in every state. For many companies, homeowner's insurance has traditionally been a profitable line, while auto insurance is a money-loser. (Despite their complaints, however, many insurers continue to profit from the car insurance business.)

The Cost Factor

Specialists called *actuaries* examine an insurer's loss experience to predict future costs—and help determine policy prices. To estimate these costs, the actuaries look at a number of different factors, including how many claims were filed in the preceding year and how high the claims were. If the insurer finds that it is receiving an increasing number of claims for serious injuries, it may attempt to impose higher premium prices on the portion of the policy that covers injuries.

Actuaries look at other relevant data. They may, for example, examine a general consumer price index or an index for a sector of the economy that relates to a particular type of insurance. The cost of a hospital room, for example, rose 9.4 percent between 1990 and 1991, according to the U.S. Department of Labor. That increase could have an impact on the portion of auto coverage related to bodily injuries. Insurers point to the escalating costs of defending auto accident liability suits as yet another growing expense that affects auto liability insurance. According to the Insurance Information Institute, an industry organization, the average liability award in a jury trial rose an average 7.6 percent each year between 1960 and 1991.

Fraud is also an issue. Insurers must consider how much they'll have to pay out each year because of deceptive medical claims or fake repair bills. According to the industry, fraud accounts for as much as 10 percent of every auto insurance premium (see page 24). Finally, there's the theft rate for autos; according to the FBI, one in 117 registered cars was stolen in 1991.

Auto repair costs, on the other hand, have been virtually stable in recent years. And damage claims for cars and other property were also stable. Yet the cost of property damage insurance rose 4.5 percent in 1992. Some activist groups, including the National Insurance Consumer Organization, have called for a nationwide rollback of auto insurance rates to correct this discrepancy.

The Territorial Factor

Auto insurance costs aren't the same everywhere in the country. To a degree, they depend on population density: Statistically, city drivers bump into each other more often than do people in less crowded areas. Our young driver with the *TransAm* lives in Detroit, where theft rates are higher than in rural or suburban areas of Michigan. Staged, fraudulent accidents also happen more frequently in urban areas than in less populated ones. On the other hand, fatalities occur more often on high-speed rural highways than on city or suburban streets.

To account for these differences, insurers break up every state into territories or zones, often along county boundaries. Not surprisingly, territories with lower-than-average repair and hospital costs, lawsuit awards, and accident rates receive cheaper rates from insurers.

The Overhead Factor

Once a company has compiled all its projected claims costs, it looks at its other expenses. How much will it have to pay for office space, supplies, advertising, taxes, salaries, and benefits? How much will it have to pay to agents on commission? According to A. M. Best Company, an insurance industry research firm, 20 cents of every auto insurance dollar goes toward such expenses. If the cost of claims adjustment is included, that overhead rises to a whopping 35 cents. That cost can vary widely, however, depending on how a company is run and how efficiently it manages expenses. Companies that don't use independent commission agents generally have lower overhead—for example, because they don't have to pay costly commissions.

All those dollars paid for premiums, by the way, don't sit around in a bank vault while the company waits for claims. Insurers invest that money in everything from government and corporate bonds to real estate. In 1991 an estimated $476.3 billion in investments originated from companies that sell auto and homeowner's insurance.

Insurers make most of their profits from investments, not from the money they collect in premiums. In these days of declining interest rates, insurers who made money before on interest income alone suddenly have had to cast about for other ways to make a profit. That usually means charging higher premiums. But in some states—New Jersey, for example—regulators have the power to tell a company to reduce its rates in a particular insurance line because the state believes the insurer is making excessive profits.

The Driver Factor

In pricing insurance, insurers also look at the types of people they insure. While some companies cover a wide demographic spectrum of drivers, others specialize in covering groups of people of the same profession or those who live in the same geographic area. The most efficient—though hardly the most fair—way to determine who will pay more and who will pay less is to create "classes" of people with similar characteristics: age, sex, marital status, and driving experience.

Consider again our young driver from Detroit. One reason he pays such a high premium is his youth. Drivers under 25—males in particular—are considered worse insurance risks than older drivers. This belief is based on fact. According to the National Safety Council, drivers under age 25 account for 29.4 percent of all accidents, although they represent only 15.6 percent of registered drivers. And the accidents they have tend to be more severe than those of older drivers. At the same time, male drivers are more than 50 percent more likely to be involved in fatal auto accidents than are female drivers. Insurers respond to these grim statistics by charging more to insure young unmarried male drivers. Our Detroit driver may be a responsible young man who drives no farther than the post office every day, but he pays a high premium for his car insurance because his demographic group has a poor track record.

Insurers also charge young drivers more because of their lack of experience. They are usually charged the highest premiums in their first three years of driving because, insurers say, they have no record to prove they're good drivers. This assumption of guilty until proven innocent can be a problem for older drivers, too. If you've been out of the country for more than three years—or if you're an immigrant with no driving history in the United States—you're likely to be charged more for insurance than your neighbor who's been here awhile. One insurer, United Services Automobile Association, was founded for that very reason: Its original customers, military officers and their dependents, couldn't get car insurance because they regularly moved from state to state or lived abroad for months and years at a time. Contrary to insurance-industry predictions, those customers turned out to be

among the safest and most responsible drivers around.

Married people often end up paying less for auto insurance than do single people. Insurers claim marital status is a good predictor of how many accidents one will have, perhaps because married people are considered more responsible and rooted in a community. Thus, a single person—particularly a male—may not gain the less-expensive "adult" coverage until he marries. Indeed, according to a publication by Allstate Insurance Company, a single male might not obtain "adult" insurance status until age 49!

The Auto Factor

Our young Detroit driver has another mark against him: his car. Insurers don't like to insure sports or performance cars such as the *TransAm*. For one, these cars often are in the shop for expensive repairs because their drivers historically, for whatever reason, have more severe accidents. Sleek and racy cars also may be stolen more often than other cars. As a result, many companies refuse to insure performance cars, or charge a very high premium if they do. (See box on pages 22–23 for a list of cars that often are difficult or impossible to insure.)

Auto insurers charge higher premiums for luxury cars, too, because they are more apt to be stolen and are more expensive to repair. According to the Highway Loss Data Institute, the most expensive car to repair in 1991 was a late-model *BMW M-3;* its overall claims cost more than five times the average. On the positive side, luxury cars often have built-in safety features, such as front-seat air bags, that can mitigate severe injuries in an accident. Insurers give points for such features by slightly lowering the driver's premiums.

Insurers often say that the least expensive cars to insure are large American station wagons and minivans. This doesn't necessarily mean they're safer, however. It does indicate that they may be cheaper to repair because their parts may be less expensive and easier to repair than those of foreign cars. Also, the people who drive them may be, on average, safer drivers than the population as a whole. The better driving experience of that group, of course, will be reflected in lower insurance rates.

Insurers take all the information they've compiled on cars and devise a car classification system every year. Each new and used car is given a number or letter corresponding to the cost of insuring it. Agents and customer service representatives refer to this list when quoting the cost of insurance. If you're choosing between two cars to buy, your choice might be made easier by having an agent check the list to see which car is cheaper to insure (see Appendix D). The box on pages 22–23 lists those cars that are difficult to insure.

The Use Factor

How and why you use a car also affects the premiums you pay. Insurers routinely ask drivers whether they use a car for commuting to and from work, for business purposes, for farming, or only for "pleasure" driving (meaning mainly weekend jaunts, shopping, etc.). Motorists pay most for business use, as when a salesperson or real estate agent uses a car as an essential part of work. The next most expensive use is commuting, followed by farming and driving for pleasure.

As shown by these cost gradations, there's a strong correlation between the likelihood of an accident and how many miles you drive each year. Some insurers charge less to people who drive under 7,500 miles annually, and they may also create another price division for customers who drive fewer than 3,000 miles a year.

The Safe Driving Factor

Another factor that influences the cost of the insurance premium is a driver's individual accident record. Those with recent histories of moving violations and *at-fault accidents*—that is, accidents for which they were found to be primarily responsible—pay much more for coverage. Indeed, drivers with bad accident histories can end up paying four times the amount that "clean" drivers pay. Every accident you have can add hundreds of dollars in surcharges to your premium, and these surcharges remain part of your insurance cost for three years or more.

The Regulatory Factor

There's another factor that influences the cost of car insurance: All states, with

HIGH- OR NO-COVERAGE CARS

The following luxury and high-performance cars are not impossible to insure, but coverage will cost far more than for other cars in their class.

MAKE	MODEL
BMW	600 Series
	700 Series
	800 Series
Chevrolet Corvette	ZR-1
Dodge	Viper
Jaguar	XJ12
	XJS
Lamborghini	Countach
	Diablo
	Jalpa
Maserati	Shamal
	Spyder
	425
	430
Mercedes-Benz	400 Series
	500 Series
	600 Series
Porsche	911
	968
	944
	928

Source: The Progressive Insurance Company

The following collectors' cars are generally ineligible for insurance:

Allard	DeTomaso
Alvis	Duesenberg
Auburn	Elegant
Avanti	Excalibur
Berlina	Lafer
Bitter	Panther
Bricklin	Scimitar
Bristol	Shelby Cobra

Chaparral	Sparks Turbo
Clenet	Stallion
Cord	Stutz
DeLorean	Zimmer

Coverage is also generally not available for all kit cars or replicas exceeding $20,000 in value. Owners must self-insure, that is, pay for any damage out of their own pocket.

Source: State Farm Insurance Company

the exception of Wyoming, regulate insurance rates. This means that in order to protect consumers, the state insurance departments may have a say in how high insurers can raise their premium rates every year. In doing so, the states consider three issues:

- Are the rates high enough to cover the company's costs and provide a reasonable profit?
- Are the rates fair, or do they discriminate against a particular demographic group?
- Are the rates excessive to the consumer?

Some states employ their own actuaries to help answer these questions, and some hold public hearings to obtain opinions from many diverse parties, including active consumer groups.

Insurance rates can be regulated by a state in the following ways:

- *Commissioner determined.* The state insurance commissioner decides every year how much rates will rise (only Massachusetts has this system).
- *Prior approval.* Every insurance company in the state must tell regulators what it wants to charge before it puts the new rates into effect. The state can veto the proposed changes or suggest amendments.
- *File and use.* Companies can go ahead and charge new rates at the same time they inform the state of their changes. The state has the right, however, to review the rates later and require changes.
- *Use and file.* This method allows insurers to charge new rates before they file those rates with the state.
- *Flex.* Companies are allowed to raise or lower their rates up to certain percentages prescribed by the state. The state only intervenes when the company tries to set rates higher or lower than the rates within this "flex band" or margin.
- *No file.* This type of regulation allows companies to charge what they like and leaves it up to the marketplace to determine whether the rates

REACTING TO THE REGULATORS

To counteract so-called inadequate rates, insurers are tightening their standards for new customers. Some drivers who previously had no trouble buying coverage now find that no company will insure them. Even one accident can prevent them from getting coverage.

Agents across the country confirm this, reporting that their companies are becoming much more selective. Whenever state regulations permit, insurers can insist that new adult applicants have at least five years' good driving experience, not just three. Insurers are also checking up on teen driving records every six months instead of every year, and some are refusing to sign up even good drivers who are in high-risk state insurance plans. They're depending more heavily on the information revealed by independent data bases, such as the Comprehensive Loss Underwriting Exchange (CLUE), which documents any claims that prospective customers may have filed with their former insurance companies.

Increasingly, insurers are not accepting new applicants in some states. Or, they are canceling policies more quickly, not allowing a grace period to drivers who don't pay on time. Some companies are even leaving states where they claim they can't make a profit, and in some cases they are abandoning the auto insurance line entirely to concentrate on other types of business.

Consumers should not worry too much if they see insurers leaving their state, however. Even in states that are unpopular with insurers, enough carriers still exist to provide choices for good drivers. Besides, insurers who leave one state to go elsewhere are often giving up very small shares of the auto insurance business in that area. Most likely, these companies weren't profitable in a particular state because they didn't maintain enough customers to create an efficient, cost-effective operation.

are fair. (Wyoming follows this system.)

Naturally, insurance companies prefer *not* having their prices reviewed by the state. The auto insurance industry claims a loss of close to $1 billion a year because of tight state regulations. Many insurers claim they can't make a profit on the rates that some states allow them to charge. But this type of rate regulation isn't as widespread as the industry insists it is. Insurers acknowledge that five states—Massachusetts, New Jersey, Pennsylvania, South Carolina, and Texas—account for most of this rate "suppression."

The Fraud Factor

As mentioned previously, a major influence on auto insurance premiums is fraud.

Let's say you're rushing home one night in your *BMW*. In fact, you're in

HOW TO PREVENT FRAUD

Insurers insist they're vigorously policing fraud. In the past few years, many companies have established special investigative units to follow up on suspicious claims and report them to state law-enforcement officials. Insurers are also starting fraud-reporting hot lines for consumers, and more aggressively training employees to spot questionable claims.

The insurance industry's critics say insurers' commitment to do anything about fraud ranges from zealous to zero. For many companies, it may be easier just to pass on the cost to consumers. Even insurers that have increased their fraud-policing efforts often let many nickel-and-dime fraud cases go unchallenged. Such laxity occurs because companies can be sued if they deny a claim but then can't actually prove the claim was fraudulent. Insurers also complain that fraud detection isn't only their job. State governments must help, they insist, through industry-financed but state-run fraud bureaus. More aggressive prosecution of fraud cases is therefore urged.

Insurers and government officials believe their real challenge is to better educate the public about spotting and avoiding fraud. This is a difficult challenge, however. Because auto insurance costs more than $1,000 per car in some places, many people feel justified in padding a claim so they can get back $500 from a $1,200 annual premium. According to a 1992 survey by the Roper Organization, some 23 percent of households interviewed said it was acceptable to pad an insurance claim to recover a collision deductible. Thirty-two percent said it was "almost always" or "usually" all right to understate their mileage on applications to save money on premiums. Twenty percent approved of telling an insurer that an older person drove a car actually being driven by someone under 21.

Why should a consumer, particularly one who feels cheated by the high cost of auto insurance, care about insurance fraud on the highway or in a body shop? Because, the industry says, the cost of that fraud returns to haunt consumers as a group in higher premiums. By one estimate, Massachusetts drivers pay $100 to $200 a year more because of auto insurance fraud.

Besides listening to your conscience, insurers and law-enforcement officers ask that you remain vigilant when you drive the nation's highways. If you are accidentally involved in a rear-end collision, you may really be an unwitting victim. To protect yourself, always keep good records of the accident. Your detailed report is helpful to fraud investigators, and it may speed up the resolution of a case.

You can also call the National Insurance Crime Bureau's (NICB) fraud hot line at 800-835-6422. In addition, your state may have a fraud hot line; check your state insurance department for details (see Appendix B).

such a hurry that you're following the *Toyota* in front of you a little too closely. A *Ford* pulls up in the lane next to you, speeds up, passes you, and cuts in front of the *Toyota*. The *Toyota* stops short. Before you can say "fender bender," you've plowed into the *Toyota*. The *Ford* that started all the trouble roars off.

This may be a routine accident. Then again, it may be staged, a ruse set up by a crime ring to win thousands of dollars from your insurance company.

In a typical staged accident, for example, a group of people cruise an upscale community looking for someone driving alone in a late-model expensive car. Using a second car, they stage an accident—perhaps a fender bender like the one just described. The people in the car you've hit insist their injuries aren't severe enough to call the police or go to the hospital. But weeks later, their attorney calls you, insisting that his clients be compensated by your insurance company for thousands of dollars in "soft-tissue" injuries, such as neck or back sprains.

In some cases, two coconspirators create the accident. They deliberately run into each other, then file claims with their auto insurers. In fact, car owners are sometimes paid off to lend their vehicles for the scam.

Auto insurance fraud isn't only committed by professional criminals or con artists. Sometimes, individuals arrange to have their cars stolen or totaled in order to collect the insurance. They may pad claims, insisting on reimbursement for unnecessary expenses. All told, the industry says, 5 to 25 percent of auto insurance claims involve some type of fraud.

SETTING THE PRICE

All of these factors are compiled, studied, and evaluated by the insurer. First, the company projects all of its costs, including the cost of paying claims in the upcoming period. Then it estimates an average rate needed for a particular coverage in a given state to cover these costs. Finally, it adjusts those rates up or down for different territories and classes of cars and drivers. That way, better risks—people who are judged to be less likely to have accidents—are generally charged lower-than-average premiums. Worse risks have to pay more.

What does all this mean to the consumer? Well, it means you can control some factors that contribute to insurance costs but not others. Certainly you can't do anything about your age, sex, or, to some degree, where you live and park your car. But other factors are under your control, including the type of car you drive and how you use it. Better driving habits (see Part II of this book) can result in fewer accidents, for example. And you can reduce your insurance bill by carefully choosing your insurance company and the extent of your coverages (see chapter 3).

You may believe that you have no control over larger trends, such as fraud, car-theft rates, and frequency of lawsuits. In fact, as a citizen, you do. Concerned motorists have lobbied aggressively—and often successfully—for better fraud and car-theft prevention measures from state governments and from the insurance industry. They've also fought for effective no-fault insurance laws, and for the repeal of laws that exempt insurers from costly noncompetitive practices. These initiatives can have a major impact on what all drivers pay for insurance.

3

Shopping the Companies

—

It's wise to check out several insurance companies before you decide on the one you want. Even drivers with an accident or a moving violation on their record may have more choices than they expect.

You won't find any bargains, but there are opportunities to trim costs considerably, often just by getting quotes over the telephone from many different insurers. In 1992, when *Consumer Reports* compared sample auto insurance premiums in 10 of the most populous states across the country, there were differences of more than 100 percent in premiums for the same type of driver, with the same coverage, in the same city. In suburban Cleveland, for example, a married couple with a teenage son could pay as much as $4,538 or as little as $1,731 to insure two cars.

WHAT KIND OF COMPANY?

Before you make a call, however, it's helpful to know the different kinds of insurers that exist in the marketplace. The most common insurers are *stock insurers,* such as The Travelers Corporation, which is owned by stockholders. Other insurers, such as State Farm, are *mutual companies* that are, in theory, owned by the policyholders. When you become a State Farm customer, you may have to pay a onetime "membership" fee, usually no more than $16.

In actual practice, large stock and mutual companies operate similarly with policyholders. Some mutual companies regularly issue dividends. You can't count on a dividend, however, just because your company is a mutual company, or because it's profitable in a given year. The dividend you receive (or don't receive) may depend on the company's financial performance in your state, not on its performance nationwide.

Most insurers, whether stock or mutual companies, employ agents to bring them new business. Some companies directly employ their agents; others use independent agents or brokers who deal with several companies, and in theory these agents can direct customers to lower-priced firms among them (see pages 42–43).

A typical agent's commission on a new auto insurance policy is 10 to 15 percent of the premium. This cost, which gets passed on in higher prices to the consumer, has influenced some companies to avoid using commission agents altogether. Such companies are called *direct writers,* because they deal with consumers directly by telephone and through the mail. The 1992 *Consumer Reports* survey found that these companies were some of the least expensive insurers. They include United Services Automobile Association (USAA) and Government Employees Insurance Company (GEICO). Theoretically, they pass on to consumers the savings they make from bypassing commission-driven agents. Many direct writers ranked high in *Consumer Reports* Ratings for service (see Appendix A).

Some insurers, including several direct writers, manage to control losses and offer low rates because they are open only to certain demographic groups. USAA and its subsidiary, USAA Casu-

alty Insurance Company, for example, serve only current and former military officers and their families, a group the company says is less often involved in accidents than the general population. That keeps USAA's premiums low. New Jersey Manufacturers Insurance Company works the same way, selling primarily to state workers and employees of New Jersey firms that are members of the New Jersey Business and Industry Association.

A few auto insurers are *reciprocal exchanges.* This means that policyholders or subscribers essentially "exchange" insurance, pooling all their premiums to pay for each other's claims. Some very large reciprocal exchanges, such as the highly rated Erie Insurance Exchange, operate essentially like a stock or mutual insurance company.

Finally, there are state-sponsored insurance systems, established mainly to insure drivers who have been rejected by private insurers. These systems are often known as *assigned-risk plans,* or pools, because the private insurers in the state are required or "assigned" to take on a certain number of motorists who can find no coverage in the regular insurance market.

IT PAYS TO SHOP: COST

The following tables list sample premiums from 10 companies in 10 of the most populous states. (Massachusetts isn't included because the state, not insurers, sets the prices.) These figures will give you an idea of how varied premium costs can be for the same coverage among different carriers. *Keep in mind that these rates date back to early 1992, and may have changed since then.* The data are useful, though, for comparing maximum and minimum premiums available to particular types of drivers.

The companies that sold the most auto policies in each of these states were asked what they would charge three hypothetical customers in suburban, urban, and rural communities—that is, nine scenarios in all. For comparison, premiums were obtained from Amica Mutual Insurance Company, the top-rated auto insurer but not a major insurance seller in those 10 states.

The companies are listed in descending Ratings order. A few companies were not rated. Where no satisfaction rating is shown, companies are listed alphabetically. (Readers whose states are not listed should be able to get a general idea of the relative prices of major insurers by referring to the box on page 36.)

The premium you will be quoted by an insurance agent or company representative will vary according to such factors as the age and type of your car, the coverage you choose, your annual mileage, and your accident record. But if a company generally has lower premiums than other insurers in your state, chances are it would charge you lower premiums, too.

Some of the companies supplied premiums for slightly different coverage, ei-
ther because of state requirements or because they don't sell exactly what was requested. Membership fees and annual dividends are not figured into the premiums, but most companies applied common discounts, such as the multicar discount. Some companies quoted only semiannual premiums; these have been doubled to arrive at an approximate annual premium. Those companies that could not or would not supply premiums are footnoted; their premiums were obtained from state insurance departments. (Premiums are as of February 15, 1992—except for Michigan and Texas, where rates are as of April 1, 1992.)

To use the tables, pick the column that reflects your area of residence—suburban, urban, or rural. Within that column, select the customer type—A, B, or C—that most closely matches you and your driving habits:

Customer A. A husband and wife, both age 41, and their 17-year-old son. The husband drives a 1991 *Honda Accord* nine miles to work and a total of 10,000 miles annually. The son drives a 1989 *Toyota Corolla* about 4,000 miles annually and is not listed on the policy as a principal operator. All have clean driving records, with no recent at-fault accidents or moving violations.

Coverages for both cars include bodily injury liability, $100,000 per person, $300,000 per accident; property damage liability, $50,000; medical payments or personal-injury protection (PIP), $5,000; collision with a $250 deductible; comprehensive with a $50 deductible; and the state's basic uninsured motorist coverage.

Customer B. A retired couple—the husband is age 62 and the wife 60. They drive a 1983 *Oldsmobile Delta 88* for pleasure only (about 4,000 miles a year). They both have clean driving records.

Coverages include: bodily injury liability, $100,000 per person, $300,000 per accident; property damage liability, $50,000; medical payments or PIP, $2,000; collision with a $100 deductible; comprehensive with no deductible; and the state's basic uninsured motorist coverage.

Customer C. A 23-year-old single male. He drives a 1992 *Pontiac Firebird TransAm* 15 miles to work, and drives a total of 20,000 miles a year. He has one chargeable accident.

Coverages include: bodily injury liability, $50,000 per person, $100,000 per accident; property damage liability, $25,000; medical payments or PIP, $2,000; collision with a $250 deductible; comprehensive coverage with a $100 deductible; and the state's basic uninsured motorist coverage.

As the tables show, it pays to shop. Yet fewer than half the respondents in the 1991 *Consumer Reports* survey of readers compared rates when they last bought insurance; of those, two-thirds called only one or two companies or agents. To save on insurance costs, it's essential to call as many companies as time allows. (Use the worksheet that follows to compare prices.)

In your search for coverage, you may not be able to compare prices exactly. Some companies, for example, offer only six-month policies instead of a full-year policy. (Double the quote to get an estimate of the annual rate.) Also insurers don't always offer the same deductibles or limits. For comparison, ask the agent or company representative for the price of coverage that's closest to what you want.

Eight states (California, Hawaii, Massachusetts, Michigan, New Hampshire, New Jersey, North Carolina, and South Carolina) have passed special legislation for good drivers—those with no claims in three years. Such individuals are entitled to buy insurance from the carrier of their choice. However, a perfect driving record may not guarantee a company's best rate. Some insurers require drivers to be with them for several years, claim-free, before they are eligible for the lowest premiums.

In most states, insurers have to give you 15 to 60 days' notice that your policy is lapsing or up for renewal. Use that time wisely. You may need all of it to find a good price. And, if the company to which you're applying has questions that need to be answered, you'll have time to answer them satisfactorily.

Don't put off shopping until the last minute; if you're caught without auto insurance for even one day, you could be subject to stiff state fines. In Nevada, for example, motorists caught driving with-

CALIFORNIA

ANNUAL PREMIUMS

Company	Overall Score	Suburban Customer			Urban Customer			Rural Customer		
		A	B	C	A	B	C	A	B	C
Amica Mutual Insurance	94	$2830	$727	$3841	$3624	$949	$4806	$2357	$581	$3403
United Services Automobile Assn.	93	1927	417	2901	2323	496	3600	1614	358	2265
USAA Casualty Insurance	91	2321	500	3506	2801	595	4351	1943	429	2736
State Farm Mutual Automobile Insurance	87	3132	486	4275	4482	728	5988	2708	396	4107
California State Automobile Assn. ①②	83	2838	936	2209	3966	1308	3052	2120	696	1624
Allstate Insurance	82	2340	672	2824 ③	3190	882	4132 ③	1674	476	2212 ③
Farmers Insurance Exchange	82	3061	651	5537 ③	4192	904	7510 ③	2419	520	4606 ③
20th Century Insurance	79	1892 ③	536	2270	2784 ③	780	3380	1626 ③	440	2070
Interinsurance Exchange of the Automobile Club of Southern California ②④	—	1973	537	2178	3565	898	4170	1794	509	1826
Mercury Insurance	—	1822	738	2754	2870	1118	4180	1860	742	2840

① *Serves northern California.*
② *Open to auto club members only.*
③ *Premiums for renewals.*
④ *Serves southern California.*

FLORIDA

ANNUAL PREMIUMS

Company	Overall Score	Suburban Customer			Urban Customer			Rural Customer		
		A	B	C	A	B	C	A	B	C
Amica Mutual Insurance	94	$2467	$654	$2950	$3484	$947	$3883	$1966	$518	$2478
United Services Automobile Assn.	93	1785	494	2209	2450	673	3224	1312	358	1688
Nationwide Mutual Fire Insurance	87	3116	757	2941	4523	1125	4344	2243	517	2307
State Farm Mutual Automobile Insurance	87	2572	584	2234	3230	710	3066	1890	384	1772
State Farm Fire & Casualty Insurance	85	3126	770	2640	3962	954	3642	2218	498	2082
Liberty Mutual Fire Insurance ①	84	3117	828	2808	3822	1126	3737	2129	568	1940
Government Employees Insurance ①	84	2208	512	2562	3575	858	3951	1661	378	1917
Allstate Insurance	82	2661	712	2558 ②	4339	1162	4350 ②	2017	544	1939 ②
Prudential Property & Casualty	80	2582	746	3062	3988	1114	4994	1856	538	2182
Allstate Indemnity ③	79	4397	1107	4709	6529	1681	7315	3243	785	3773

① *Passive-restraint discount not included.*
② *Premiums for renewals.*
③ *Writes insurance mainly for high-risk drivers.*

ILLINOIS

ANNUAL PREMIUMS

Company	Overall Score	Suburban Customer			Urban Customer			Rural Customer		
		A	B	C	A	B	C	A	B	C
Amica Mutual Insurance	94	$2961	$871	$4468	$4264	$1238	$7079	$1735	$530	$2707
State Farm Mutual Automobile Insurance	87	2406	436	2930	2812	528	3312	1408	244	1898
Country Mutual Insurance	86	2331	524	①	3266	720	①	1330	283	①
American Family Mutual Insurance	86	3146	682	3559 ②	3670	813	4082 ②	1984	415	2410 ②
State Farm Fire & Casualty Insurance	85	2870	660	3310	3400	812	3764	1674	368	2158
Illinois Farmers Insurance	85	2397	537	4822 ②	2184	506	4793 ②	999	226	2356 ②
Allstate Insurance	82	1938	443	3069 ②	2838	689	4361 ②	1448	321	2459 ②
American Ambassador Casualty ③④	—	3781	1258	5854	4522	1507	7321	⑤	⑤	⑤
Economy Fire & Casualty	—	2750	652	4372	3976	920	6642	1622	364	2632
Safeway Insurance ③	—	4089	1036	10,359	5250	1270	12,917	⑤	⑤	⑤

① *Customer C ineligible for coverage.*
② *Premiums for renewals.*
③ *Writes insurance mainly for high-risk drivers.*
④ *Premiums supplied by state insurance department. Discounts not included.*
⑤ *No information available.*

MARYLAND

ANNUAL PREMIUMS

Company	Overall Score	Suburban Customer			Urban Customer			Rural Customer		
		A	B	C	A	B	C	A	B	C
Amica Mutual Insurance	94	$2880	$755	$3897	$4310	$1167	$5486	$2046	$530	$3008
United Services Automobile Assn. [1]	93	1713	480	2279	2145	603	2794	1220	331	1767
Erie Insurance Exchange	88	2287	518	2894 [2]	2947	671	3628 [1]	1357	299	1904 [1]
State Farm Mutual Automobile Insurance	87	2480	566	2716	3468	800	3628	1690	354	2092
State Farm Fire & Casualty Insurance	85	3216	788	3622	4496	1114	4842	2180	494	2790
Nationwide Mutual Insurance	85	2798	745	3298	4779	1306	5333	1179	455	2249
Liberty Mutual Fire Insurance [1]	84	2778	680	2704	3932	965	3672	1662	401	1728
Government Employees Insurance [1]	84	1760	399	2304	3035	705	3745	1635	357	2362
Allstate Insurance	82	2156	532	2958 [1]	3486	902	4386 [1]	1670	395	2527 [1]
Allstate Indemnity [3]	79	4183	1108	4830	7480	2098	7602	3280	836	4316

[1] Passive-restraint discount not included.   [3] Writes insurance primarily for high-risk drivers.
[2] Premiums for renewals.

MICHIGAN

ANNUAL PREMIUMS [1]

Company	Overall Score	Suburban Customer			Urban Customer			Rural Customer		
		A	B	C	A	B	C	A	B	C
Amica Mutual Insurance	94	$2528	$754	$3501	$2788	$805	$3988	$1933	$612	$2519
Auto-Owners Insurance	89	2360	596	5933	2713	674	6904	1701	447	4140
Citizens Insurance Co. of America [2]	89	2588	633	2891	3819	927	4913	2175	543	2408
State Farm Mutual Automobile Insurance	87	2726	656	2918	2930	702	3128	2202	560	2238
Transamerica Insurance	86	3806	806	3738	4324	856	4308	2670	598	2596
Auto Club Insurance Assn. [3] [4]	83	2216	596	2684	4964	1254	6258	2216	596	2684
Allstate Insurance	82	2647	1030	3032	3384	1307	3951	2122	827	2427
Farmers Insurance Exchange	82	2715	777	8271	3007	855	9177	1813	537	5462
Auto Club Group Insurance [3] [4]	—	1994	536	2416	4468	1129	5632	1994	536	2416
MIC General Insurance [5]	—	2635	639	2961	4886	1062	8295	2059	475	2489

[1] Premiums include Michigan Catastrophic Claims Assn. fee.   [4] Open only to auto club members and employees of large companies.
[2] Premiums as of May 14, 1992.   [5] Open only to employees of General Motors Corp. and other large companies.
[3] Premiums are from before April 1, 1992.

NEW JERSEY

ANNUAL PREMIUMS [1]

Company	Overall Score	Suburban Customer			Urban Customer			Rural Customer		
		A	B	C	A	B	C	A	B	C
Amica Mutual Insurance	94	$2992	$836	$3756	$3723	$1028	$4924	$2871	$806	$3655
United Services Automobile Assn.	93	2501	754	3331	3044	902	4248	2358	713	3180
New Jersey Manufacturers Insurance [2]	89	2381	712	2717	3131	910	3800	2366	718	2685
State Farm Mutual Automobile Insurance	87	2938	682	3098	4058	922	4132	3138	738	3198
Liberty Mutual Fire Insurance [2]	84	2333	710	2742	3104	918	3605	2414	744	2780
Allstate Insurance	82	3226	794	3641 [3]	3940	924	4557 [3]	3096	759	3539 [3]
First Trenton Indemnity [4]	—	2838	874	2450	3330	974	3252	2696	810	2410
Moter Club of America Insurance [2][5]	—	3325	877	4106	4141	1219	5258	3127	866	3929
Prudential Property & Casualty Insurance Co. of New Jersey	—	2836	1074	3974	3466	1280	5044	2654	1014	3768
Selective Insurance Co. of America	—	3030	895	3116	3591	1042	3653	2850	848	2967

[1] All premiums reflect New Jersey's lawsuit-limitation option.   [4] Formerly Travelers Insurance Co.
[2] Passive-restraint discount not included.   [5] Formerly MCA Insurance Co.
[3] Premiums for renewals.

NEW YORK   ANNUAL PREMIUMS

Company	Overall Score	Suburban Customer			Urban Customer			Rural Customer		
		A	B	C	A	B	C	A	B	C
Amica Mutual Insurance	94	$3236	$922	$5100	$5221	$1393	$9367	$1923	$548	$2759
State Farm Mutual Automobile Insurance	87	3154	712	3882	4938	1064	6170	1650	372	1938
Nationwide Mutual Insurance	85	3270	824	3698	4978	1313	6285	1861	493	2022
Liberty Mutual Fire Insurance [1]	84	3208	845	3350	5142	1291	5929	1785	470	1807
Government Employees Insurance [1]	84	2523	685	3558	3532	912	4733	1474	427	1909
Allstate Insurance	82	3497	920	5038 [2]	4238	1046	6164 [2]	1618	482	1906 [2]
Travelers Indemnity [3]	80	2758	770	3214	5234	1370	6606	1564	450	1886
Automobile Insurance Co. of Hartford [4]	—	2880	866	4518	4078	1114	6406	1572	488	2290
General Accident Insurance Co. of New York	—	3935	813	4057	6948	1253	7586	2508	458	2399
New York Central Mutual Fire Insurance	—	2285	544	3527	5105	808	8085	1491	313	2263

[1] *Passive-restraint discount not included.*   [3] *Customers A and B would be placed with Phoenix Insurance Co.*
[2] *Premiums for renewals.*   [4] *Premiums from state insurance department. Discounts not included.*

OHIO   ANNUAL PREMIUMS [1]

Company	Overall Score	Suburban Customer			Urban Customer			Rural Customer		
		A	B	C	A	B	C	A	B	C
Amica Mutual Insurance	94	$2341	$602	$3577	$1976	$500	$2852	$1655	$416	$2498
Cincinnati Insurance	93	2763	585	3942	1908	419	2553	1695	367	2445
Nationwide Mutual Fire Insurance	87	1731	476	2306	1558	421	2064	1447	387	1973
State Farm Mutual Automobile Insurance	87	2104	408	3178	1626	318	2342	1712	316	2456
State Automobile Mutual Insurance	85	4538	586 [3]	7411 [4]	2776	362 [3]	4265 [4]	2466	308 [3]	4133 [4]
State Farm Fire & Casualty Insurance	85	2760	594	3858	2122	462	2836	2176	458	2980
Nationwide Mutual Insurance [2]	85	1924	529	2562	1731	469	2294	1607	431	2192
Allstate Insurance	82	2626	654	3712 [4]	1536	360	2122 [4]	1486	346	2166 [4]
Grange Mutual Casualty	—	2184	612	3188	2258	622	3442	1810	498	2808
Motorists Mutual Insurance	—	3044	594	6057	2148	432	4043	1724	342	3356

[1] *Suburban premiums are for suburban Cleveland and urban rates are for Cincinnati, resulting in higher suburban rates.*
[2] *Available in Ohio only to farm bureau members.*   [4] *Premiums for renewals.*
[3] *Placed with State Auto Property & Casualty Co.*

PENNSYLVANIA   ANNUAL PREMIUMS [1]

Company	Overall Score	Suburban Customer			Urban Customer			Rural Customer		
		A	B	C	A	B	C	A	B	C
Amica Mutual Insurance	94	$3201	$888	$3373	$4767	$1331	$4941	$2014	$550	$2229
Erie Insurance Exchange	88	2357	735	3665 [2]	4089	1305	6125 [2]	1176	338	2244 [2]
Erie Insurance Co.	87	3429	1063	5150 [2]	5801	1831	8466 [2]	1854	512	3372 [2]
State Farm Mutual Automobile Insurance	87	2674	644	2588	4326	1080	4038	1690	370	1816
State Farm Fire & Casualty Insurance	85	3462	814	3480	5600	1362	5424	2124	466	2274
Nationwide Mutual Insurance	85	3298	834	4063	7527	2061	8564	2630	651	3480
Liberty Mutual Fire Insurance [3]	84	2861	789	2688	3314	902	3142	1513	418	1581
Allstate Insurance	82	2249	579	2524 [2]	6045	1809	5912 [2]	1751	456	2163 [2]
Prudential Property & Casualty Insurance	80	2352	835	4441	4462	1621	7896	1204	404	2590
Pennland Insurance [4]	—	3329	1040	3355	5466	1718	6815	2245	671	3217

[1] *All premiums reflect Pennsylvania's tort liability option.*   [3] *Passive-restraint discount not included.*
[2] *Premiums for renewals.*   [4] *No discounts included in premiums.*

TEXAS

Company	Overall Score	Suburban Customer			Urban Customer			Rural Customer		
		A	B	C	A	B	C	A	B	C
Amica Mutual Insurance	94	$2431	$633	$2388	$2604	$682	$2576	$1830	$495	$2009
United Services Automobile Assn.	93	2194	523	1985	2382	565	2150	1657	403	1680
State Farm Mutual Automobile Insurance [1]	87	2560	578	2332	2758	624	2514	1940	462	1962
Allstate Insurance	82	2942	722	2340 [2]	3494	854	2742 [2]	2222	558	2002 [2]
Allstate Indemnity	79	2702	554	2344 [2]	2942	616	2538 [2]	2014	422	1966 [2]
Allstate County Mutual [3]	—	4512	1070	8290	5715	1387	10381	4136	910	9358
Mid-Century Insurance Co. of Texas [4]	—	2822	520	2602 [2]	3040	578	2776 [2]	2104	410	2228 [2]
Southern Farm Bureau Casualty Insurance [5]	—	2560	520	3020	2842	554	3322	2024	370	2488
State & County Mutual Fire Insurance [3][6]	—	3887	1102	3508	4875	1339	4474	3031	878	2805
State Farm County Mutual Insurance Co. of Texas	—	3376	898	3148	3652	972	3394	2570	712	2636

[1] *Premiums as of May 1, 1992.*
[2] *Premiums for renewals.*
[3] *Writes insurance mainly for high-risk drivers.*
[4] *Young driver insured with Texas Farmers Insurance Co.*
[5] *Open to farm-bureau members only.*
[6] *Premiums obtained from state insurance department. Discounts not included.*

INSURANCE SHOPPER'S WORKSHEET

	Write amount of coverage here	Write premiums from each company in these columns		
		COMPANY 1	COMPANY 2	COMPANY 3
How much coverage do you want?				
1. Bodily injury liability				
2. Property damage liability				
3. Uninsured motorist				
4. Underinsured motorist				
5. Medical payments				
6. Personal-injury protection (no-fault states)				
7. Collision				
a. $100 deductible				
b. $250 deductible				
c. $500 deductible				
d. $1000 deductible				
8. Comprehensive				
a. No deductible				
b. $50 deductible				
c. $100 deductible				
d. $250 deductible				
e. $500 deductible				
Subtotal A:				
Other charges or discounts				
Membership fees				
Surcharges				
Discounts				
Subtotal B:				
Subtotal A plus Subtotal B equals your **TOTAL PREMIUM**				

WHO'S HIGH? WHO'S LOW?

Based on state-by-state data, these insurers' premiums were significantly lower or higher than average. Scores taken from Ratings of auto insurers (see Appendix A).

LOW PREMIUMS	SCORE
United Services Automobile Association (USAA)	93
Erie Insurance Exchange	88
State Farm Mutual	87
Nationwide Mutual	85
Government Employees (GEICO)	84
Liberty Mutual Fire	84
Allstate	82
Prudential Property & Casualty	80
HIGH PREMIUMS	
Farmers Insurance Exchange	82
Allstate Indemnity	79

out insurance are subject to fines of $300 to $1,000. In Wyoming, the penalty is up to $750 or six months in jail. In Pennsylvania, uninsured motorists can have their licenses and registrations revoked.

IT PAYS TO SHOP: SERVICE

Price may be foremost in shopping for auto insurance, but service is crucial if you're ever in an accident and need to file a claim. How quickly does the company respond to your initial calls and claim? Is payment of your claim prompt and without problems? Nearly 257,000 readers of *Consumer Reports* answered questions related to their auto insurance experiences in a 1991 survey. It included some 63,000 consumers who had filed a claim in the previous three years, enough to supply at least 200 claim experiences for each of the companies rated (and many more for the biggest companies). While the list certainly doesn't include all auto insurers, it does include many major carriers.

Just as the high-rated companies seem to provide good service consistently, many of the lower-rated companies seem to have a consistent record of relatively poor service. Overall, 17 percent of all *Consumer Reports* readers who filed claims between January 1988 and the summer of 1991 reported one or more problems in settling those claims. (See Appendix A for results of a 1991 survey on overall reader satisfaction with claims handling.)

THE SHOPPING PROCESS

Trying to get the best company and policy for your money requires persistence and some knowledge of insurance procedures. You also should be aware that companies will want to know a few things about you, too.

Checking out the Applicant

Prospective insurance companies will ask you many pertinent questions, including where you live, the type of car you own, how it is used, your driving record, and any other factors that might influence their decision to sign you up as a customer. Some companies also rely on agents to check out potential customers for signs of "instability," such as frequent job changes or unusual working hours. If an insurer deems you a borderline case, it may rely on the personal impression you make on a company representative. It's difficult to predict how an agent will react, but it's safe to assume that a fairly conservative appearance, if you're meeting an agent face-to-face, might tip the balance in your favor.

You're still vulnerable to company rules and regulations, even if an insurer accepts you as a customer. The insurer has a period of time, which varies by state, to review your driving record and decide whether or not to keep you. During that period, it can cancel your coverage for any reason. So it's important to be as accurate as possible on your application. If you're caught in an error, coverage could be canceled.

If you don't remember all the details of your automobile insurance history, you can obtain a copy of your past insurance claims record from the Comprehensive Loss Underwriting Exchange (CLUE), a subsidiary of Equifax Inc., the credit-reporting agency based in Atlanta. A printout that lists all your reported auto insurance claims for the past five years is available for a fee of about $8. It does not include your record of motor vehicle violations; that information is typically kept by law-enforcement officials.

Companies often examine CLUE reports when deciding whether to insure someone. But these reports are not infallible and errors can occur. If, for example, your brother had an at-fault accident while driving your car, you could be incorrectly cited as being at fault. Be sure to let the insurer and CLUE know if your report contains an error, and insist on having it corrected. Such a mistake can affect your ability to get coverage.

CLUE will send you a copy of your report, free of charge, if you are informed by your insurer about a problem with your driving record that precludes accepting you as a customer. For such a report, contact Equifax Insurance Consumer Center, P.O. Box 105108, Atlanta, GA 30348-5108; telephone 800-456-6004 from 8 A.M. to 7 P.M. eastern time.

Varieties of Insurers: Subsidiaries

Both you and your neighbor may be offered auto insurance by the same company, but this doesn't mean you're both going to be insured by the same company. Large insurers split their business into divisions or subsidiaries with similar names, each serving a different type of driver. If you have a perfect driving record, for example, and fit the right demographic profile, you could be eligible for a company's *preferred* subsidiary. Generally, those premiums are the lowest that the company offers. To qualify, drivers need to have a perfect driving record for three to five years. (Single male drivers under age 30 usually are not eligible for the preferred category, regardless of their driving records.)

Even drivers with a pristine driving history may not be admitted to the preferred subsidiary if they've been with an insurer for only a short time. They may be directed first to the *standard subsidiary,* which offers somewhat higher premiums. Average drivers—even those with just one accident on their record— are also usually directed to the standard subsidiary.

High-risk drivers with too many traffic violations and accidents, and inexperienced drivers as well, often can only find coverage with a *nonstandard subsidiary,* or with a stand-alone company that only covers nonstandard drivers. (In Texas, unregulated insurers, known as *county mutuals,* also serve nonstandard drivers.) If you're in this category, you'll probably be paying the least attractive rates and be charged heavy penalties for any new accidents that occur after you've been signed up.

It's not always easy to tell whether you've been placed in a preferred, standard, or nonstandard subsidiary; the names can be confusing. Allstate Insurance Company, for example, insures standard drivers, whereas Allstate Indemnity Company is a "specialty," or nonstandard, insurer intended mainly for high-risk drivers.

If you don't know which is your subsidiary, or if you think you deserve to be in a better one, ask your agent or customer service representative how you can qualify. Even if you "belong" in the higher-priced subsidiary, you don't have to stay there indefinitely. If your driving record improves over time, the company could promote you to a better subsidiary. Or, you may find another insurer that offers better rates without the wait.

Agents also have been known to place unsuspecting customers in more expensive subsidiaries because they make higher commissions on the higher premiums. A professor found he had been with the more expensive subsidiary for years, although his driving record was perfect. When he asked his agent why he hadn't been moved to the better subsidiary, the agent replied, "Well, you never asked."

If you can't get coverage with a private insurance company, you're still eligible for the state high-risk or shared-risk plan. Insurers, agents, state regulators, and consumer activists say candidates for high-risk plans are usually drivers who are very young, who are new to the United States, who speak English poorly, who have had too many accidents, or who own performance or luxury cars that are difficult to insure (see box on pages 22–23). Rates for these plans can be many times the preferred rate. Even among those insurers, however, there may be choices. A state high-risk plan usually charges more than a private, nonstandard company, but not always.

If you are insured by a high-risk plan or nonstandard company and don't have any accidents or violations for three years or more, you may be accepted by a less costly standard insurer. (See chapter 5 for other strategies for staying out of state high-risk plans.)

Switching Carriers

If your auto insurance company ranks in the top half of the Ratings (see Appendix A), it's probably not worthwhile to switch to another one for minor improvements in quality of service. It's likely that you'd be judged more harshly for accidents and traffic violations as a new customer than as a longtime one.

And although it's always good to shop around, you probably won't find cheaper coverage if you've had a recent accident. However, if you've had no accidents in three years and the cost of your premium is still increasing, it may be the right time to look elsewhere for less expensive coverage.

CONSIDER THE COMPANY

An insurance company, like other commercial enterprises, is vulnerable to downturns and changes in the marketplace. For this reason, it doesn't hurt to check out the financial background and condition of any carrier you choose to do business with.

Is the Company Financially Secure?

In the 1980s, the savings-and-loan crisis was a major source of concern for Americans: Would their hard-earned money be lost? In the 1990s, the well-publicized financial problems of some insurers are raising a similar question: Will the money be there when I need it?

For buyers of auto insurance, the answer is probably yes. As of this writing, most problem insurers are in the life insurance area, not the property and casualty business, which includes auto and homeowner's insurance. And most property and casualty insurers haven't invested heavily in the type of risky financial deals that have caused the collapse of some life insurers.

AUTO INSURANCE SHOPPING GUIDES

Thirty-seven states plus the District of Columbia publish and distribute auto insurance shopping guides for residents. Most of these publications are free. A few merely tell you which coverages are required by law and what your consumer rights are. Many, though, give detailed and updated information on how much the major insurers in a state charge particular types of drivers in different counties or regions.

A few states even publish complaint rates against insurers, so consumers can see which insurance companies received the most consumer complaints during the previous year. If you would like one of these guides, contact your state insurance department (see Appendix B).

The following states offer auto insurance shopping guides:

Alaska	Kansas†	Oklahoma†
Arizona	Louisiana	Oregon
Arkansas	Maine	Pennsylvania
California*	Maryland	South Carolina
Colorado	Massachusetts†	Texas
Connecticut	Michigan	Utah
Delaware	Minnesota	Vermont
District of Columbia	Missouri	Virginia
Florida†	Nevada	Washington
Georgia‡	New Jersey	West Virginia
Hawaii	New York	Wisconsin
Illinois§	North Dakota	Wyoming†
Indiana†	Ohio	

*Telephone data base is in development.
†No premium comparisons are included.
‡Guide is in development.
§Guide isn't in printed form. Consumers must call the state insurance department to consult a computer data base for premium comparison.

Auto and homeowner's-insurance companies, however, often confront another problem: natural disasters. If a company is exposed to an unexpected number of claims following a hurricane, earthquake, or some other catastrophe, it may find itself short of funds. In 1992, Hurricane Andrew left an unprecedented $15.5 billion of damages in its wake, mainly in the state of Florida. By the end of the year, 10 small insurance companies with substantial claims from the hurricane had been declared insolvent, and still more insolvencies are expected. Ironically, those Florida insurers hadn't properly insured *themselves* against the unexpected.

In the unlikely event your auto insurance company runs into trouble, don't panic. Every state has a property and casualty guaranty fund that essentially provides insurance on your insurance. If your company is licensed in the state and becomes insolvent, most of these funds would pay your claims—or any liability claims against you—up to a limit, usually $300,000.

What happens if there is a larger claim against you—as can occur in some liability cases? You could run into problems getting money from a state guaranty fund. What's more, if the state fund itself is stretched to its limit, you could get even less. Florida's guaranty fund, for example, was insufficient to cover the claims left by Hurricane Andrew; the state had to issue bonds to make up the difference.

The best strategy to protect yourself is to choose your company wisely. A financially strong property and casualty insurer will have adequate protection against the fiscal drain of major catastrophes. So once you've selected a company for its price and quality, check out its financial status. Many libraries have ratings directories from the four major insurance company evaluation groups that cover property and casualty companies: A. M. Best, Moody's, Standard &

Poor's, and Duff & Phelps. The directories list insurers operating in the United States and rate them according to their financial stability and general fiscal condition. (Because these companies don't use the same rating system, use the following box as a source for comparison.)

Working with Insurance Agents and Brokers

No matter what the ads say about agents as "good neighbors," remember this: Insurance agents are salespeople. Their main job is to sell, not to provide service to policyholders. Agents and brokers may be useful if you have a problem claim, but their primary goal is to generate revenue for the companies they represent.

A typical independent insurance agent earns a 15 percent commission on the premium on a new policy and 12 to 15 percent each year the motorist renews the policy. In other words, the more money you pay for the coverage, the more goes into the agent's pocket. This cost of doing business is passed on wholly or partially in the cost of your premium.

For this reason, direct-writing companies that solicit business through word of mouth, telemarketing, or direct mail often have cheaper-than-average prices. Even more compelling, as we've stated elsewhere, many of the companies top-rated for service in *Consumer Reports'* Ratings are direct writers. (The Comments section of the Ratings in Appendix A indicates which companies sell only by mail or telephone.)

RATING THE INSURERS

The financial community judges the viability of auto insurers through ratings established by four different companies: A. M. Best Company, Standard & Poor's Corporation, Duff & Phelps Credit Rating Company, and Moody's Investors Service. To some degree, consumers also can use these ratings to judge the risk of buying from one insurer versus another.

Each ratings company has its own set of letter-based ratings. The ratings, although similar on the surface, can differ considerably in meaning. As the comparison below shows, an "A−" can be considered a fairly good rating from A. M. Best but not from Standard & Poor's or Moody's.

What's a consumer to do? To play it safe, choose only auto insurers with tip-top ratings—usually from the first or second row—from at least two of the four companies. The insurer can provide the ratings information, but the ratings services will also provide it free, for the cost of a telephone call (that way, you know it's up-to-date). Your local library may also have current ratings, published in large reference books. Be sure to ask for the ratings of property and casualty companies, not life and health insurers, which often have very similar names.

The ratings companies can also supply complete reports on each insurer, for a fee. Or, you may be able to obtain a report, free of charge, from your insurance agent. The typical consumer, however, probably won't find these reports particularly useful.

RATINGS USED BY A. M. BEST, STANDARD & POOR'S, MOODY'S, AND DUFF & PHELPS

RATINGS

RANK	BEST	S&P*	MOODY'S	D&P
1	A++	AAA	Aaa	AAA
2	A+	AA+	Aa1	AA+
3	A	AA	Aa2	AA
4	A−	AA−	Aa3	AA−
5	B++	A+	A1	A+
6	B+	A	A2	A
7	B	A−	A3	A−
8	B−	BBB+	Baa1	BBB+
9	C++	BBB	Baa2	BBB
10	C+	BBB−	Baa3	BBB−
11	C	BB+	Ba1	BB+
12	C−	BB	Ba2	BB
13	D	BB−	Ba3	BB−
14	E	B+	B1	B+

RATINGS

RANK	BEST	S&P*	MOODY'S	D&P
15	F	B	B2	B
16		B−	B3	B−
17		CCC+	Caa	CCC+
18		CCC	Ca	CCC
19		CCC−	C	CCC−
20		CC		
21		C		
22		D		

*S & P gives a rating of "R" to companies under regulatory supervision, after rehabilitation, receivership, liquidation, or any other action reflecting regulatory concern about an insurer's financial condition. S & P also gives qualified solvency ratings to some companies. These ratings are based solely on public information, not on data supplied by the company to Standard & Poor's.
Source: The Insurance Forum, Standard & Poor's Corporation.

ADDRESSES

A. M. Best Company
Ambest Road
Oldwick, NJ 08858
Reports: $20 each
Ratings are available through a "900" telephone number (you pay $2.50 per minute). For more information, call A. M. Best at 908-439-2200.

Standard & Poor's Corporation
25 Broadway
New York, NY 10004
212-208-1592, ext. 1527
Reports: $25 each
Ratings available free of charge.

Duff & Phelps Credit Rating
  Company
55 East Monroe Street
Chicago, IL 60603
312-368-3157
Reports: $25 each
Ratings available free of charge.

Moody's Investors Service
99 Church Street
New York, NY 10277
212-553-1658
Ratings available free of charge at 212-553-0377.

If your insurance situation is problematical, or you want face-to-face service, you have the choice of visiting an independent agent, an exclusive agent, or a broker. *Independent agents* or *brokers* represent several companies, so theoretically they can help you shop for the cheapest coverage. In practice, however, independent agents may seek to place you with the company that provides them with the best commission or incentive. An independent agent also won't shop for the right policy for you as exhaustively and thoroughly as you can yourself. Many send most of their business to just one or two companies, mainly because it's costly and more inconvenient to maintain relationships with many different insurers. If you use an independent agent, be sure to ask how many companies he or she represents.

Exclusive agents work for one company. They can quote you a price only for the insurer they represent. However, often that price can be lower than what other companies charge, in part because exclusive agents are usually paid smaller commissions than are independent agents.

If you prefer to use an agent or broker instead of a direct writer, consider getting a quote from a direct writer anyway. Then ask the agent if that price can be beat.

4

Deductibles, Discounts, and Waivers

—

Finding a company that offers good service is only your starting point in insurance shopping. Then comes the matter of cost—nearly identical coverage from different insurers can vary by thousands of dollars annually.

Why is the range so wide? It depends to some degree on each insurer's business strategy. A company interested in serving a particular segment of the market may price its policies to attract those drivers or to discourage others. It also depends on how efficient a company is. Insurers that control their overhead costs can afford to offer lower premiums than those that don't.

When shopping among companies, be sure to ask each one to give you rates for comparable coverages. The insurers may have slightly different rules—a higher minimum collision deductible, for example—but you'll get a general idea of how their prices compare.

There are other ways to save money on insurance premiums. Some make only a small dent in costs, while others can save you a significant amount of money.

CUTTING INSURANCE COSTS

No matter which company you choose, you can usually save money by taking any of the following steps.

Raise Your Deductibles

This is one of the most common ways to save money on auto insurance. Raising the collision deductible from $200 to $500 can save 15 to 30 percent on that coverage. A driver of a midsize Chevrolet in a suburban area of New York State, for example, would save about $160 annually with a $500 deductible. Raising the deductible from $500 to $1,000 would save an additional $140 a year. The most common deductible is around $250. As with collision coverage, raising your comprehensive deductible can also save money.

Most people come out ahead by taking a higher deductible, since the average driver files a collision claim only once every 10 years.

Drop Collision Coverage on Older Cars

Insurers won't pay claims beyond a car's actual cash value or market value, so collision insurance isn't worth keeping on an older car that has depreciated considerably. A common rule of thumb is to drop the coverage after four or five years, or when the collision premium equals 10 percent of the car's market value. You can check your car's value by using Consumer Reports Used Car Price Service (see page 152) or price books such as the "Blue Book" published by the National Automobile Dealers Association (most versions are actually orange). It's available in insurance offices, bank loan departments, and public libraries.

You may want to hold on to comprehensive coverage a little longer, especially if you live in a high-crime area. If your car is stolen, at least you'll get some money back to apply toward a new car.

Ask for Discounts

Companies offer many different discounts that can lower your insurance premiums, including some that are mandated by the state. Recently, New York State investigated and exposed 70 insurers that owed motorists more than $38 million in state-mandated discounts for safety and antitheft devices (see box on page 49). In some instances, the insurance company may have already included a discount in your premium. Mature-driver discounts, for example, are often already part of the premium.

Shop for a low overall premium first. Then ask about the following discounts to make certain you get the very lowest price to which you're entitled. Sometimes the discounts apply to the entire premium and sometimes just to a portion of it.

- *Defensive-driving course.* This discount allows you, as an adult, to receive from 5 to 10 percent off most coverages if you have completed a state-approved course. Mandated in 32 states and the District of Columbia, it frequently applies only to people age 55 and over.
- *Auto/homeowner's package.* Consolidating your homeowner's policy together with your auto insurance can get you anywhere from 5 to 15 percent off both policies when both are with the same company.
- *Multicar.* Insurers say that covering more than one vehicle on the same policy saves them processing costs, which they then can pass on to consumers. If the policy covers more than one car, expect to pay from 10 to 25 percent less for liability, collision, medical payments, and per-

sonal-injury protection (PIP) than you would have paid to insure each car on a separate policy.

- *Good driver/renewal.* This discount will take from 5 to 10 percent off your premium, if you qualify. You must have maintained a good driving record for at least two years (one or no at-fault accidents or traffic violations) and must have been with the same insurer for several years.
- *Mature driver.* This discount often starts at age 50 and may apply only to retired drivers. You can save usually 5 to 15 percent off most coverages. (This discount may already be included in your premium.)
- *Automatic safety belts and air bags.* Discounts for one or both of these safety features are mandated in Florida, New York, Pennsylvania, and Texas. You can receive from 10 to 30 percent off the medical payments or the personal-injury protection (PIP) portion of the premium for automatic safety belts, and from 20 to 60 percent off the same coverages for one or two air bags. (All 1991 and later cars have either automatic safety belts or at least one air bag.)
- *Antitheft devices.* Installation of alarm systems and other antitheft devices can save from 5 to 50 percent off the comprehensive part of the policy for approved devices. You must provide proof of purchase and installation. This discount is mandated in Florida, Illinois, Kentucky, Massachusetts, Michigan, New

Jersey, New York, Pennsylvania, Rhode Island, and Washington.
- *Antilock brakes.* Installation of antilock brakes generally saves from 5 to 10 percent off medical, liability, and collision coverages. This discount is mandated in Florida and New York.
- *Student driver training.* This discount, available to high school students, typically offers 10 percent off the total premium.
- *Good student.* Generally, a high school or college student must show proof of a B average or better to obtain this discount. It offers from 5 to 25 percent off most coverages.
- *Student away at school.* During the school year, the student must be residing more than 100 miles from the family home. (Insurers assume the student doesn't have frequent access to the family car.) This discount allows from 10 to 40 percent off most portions of the premium.
- *Car pool.* When drivers certify that their car is used in a car pool for commuting, they may receive from 5 to 25 percent off the total premium. However, some insurers allow this discount only if at least two other cars are included in the pool.

Choose the Car That's Cheaper to Insure

As mentioned previously, insurers consider some cars less risky—and less costly to insure—than others. If you're buying a car and the choice comes down to two models, ask an insurance agent which costs less to insure (see Appendix D).

Drive Less

Insurers usually ask all applicants how much they think they will drive in the coming year. If you use your car only for pleasure, you may be able to save some money here. Driving less than 7,500 miles a year (if your personal or professional situation permits it) will generally mean slightly lower rates.

Drive the Buick Often, the Porsche Rarely

As mentioned before, a luxury or performance car can be costly to insure. In fact, many preferred and standard companies may refuse to insure it (see pages 22–23). If you do own such a car, putting fewer miles on it (generally 7,500 miles a year or less) can help keep your rates within reason. Some manufacturers and car clubs, such as the Porsche Club of America, have special arrangements with insurers that sell coverage for luxury or performance cars. Don't assume, however, that such plans offer the cheapest coverage.

Cancel Collision While on Long Vacations

If your car is to be garaged for a month or longer, you can arrange with some insurers to have the collision and liability coverage dropped—and the premium reduced by an appropriate amount—for that period. (Check with your state's motor vehicle department about the rules, however; you may have to surrender your license plates during the hiatus.)

Consider Opting for the Lawsuit Limitation

Accident victims who win a lawsuit are often awarded money to pay their medical bills and to compensate them for nonmedical costs, or "pain and suffering." Insurers say pain-and-suffering awards are a chief factor in increased costs, which are then passed on to consumers in higher premiums.

Most states with no-fault auto insurance laws limit any suits for pain and suffering to specific cases. Kentucky, New Jersey, and Pennsylvania give motorists a choice: Keep your option to sue for pain and suffering, or agree to sue only in cases involving serious injuries or death. Consumers who choose the latter no-fault option can save an average of $225 per vehicle annually in New Jersey and $150 in Pennsylvania. In Kentucky, however, the savings are minimal.

Opt for "Unstacked" Coverage

In many states, drivers with more than one car can buy uninsured and underinsured motorist coverage for each car they own. This is known in insurance lingo as *stacking*. It means, for example, that if your uninsured-motorist coverage is $10,000 on each of two cars, you can claim up to $20,000 with your insurer when you make a single uninsured motorist claim. In Pennsylvania and Florida, however, you can choose to buy less-expensive uninsured- and underinsured-motorist coverage—if you're willing to waive the ability to "stack" coverage to obtain higher liability limits. This insurance option effectively covers multiple cars but can save you some money on the premium.

Insure Teenagers on the Family Policy

Teenagers generally pay more if they have their own auto insurance policies. If your children still live with you, you may save money overall by putting them on your policy. Indicate to the insurer which car the teenager drives; some companies will assign the higher rate for teens only to that car, which can save money on the total premium. Be sure to alert your insurer if your child is eligible for the driver-training or good-student discounts (see previous pages).

Some parents buy teens separate policies to avoid accident surcharges on their own policies; however, even with a separate policy you could still be liable if your child is sued.

DOES YOUR INSURER OWE YOU A REFUND?

If your car is equipped with air bags, automatic seat belts, or an antitheft device, you may be entitled to a discount on your auto insurance. Many insurers offer these discounts voluntarily, although such discounts are required by law in several states.

In 1991 the office of the attorney general of New York State discovered that insurers were giving mandated discounts to as few as one in five eligible drivers. Officials estimated that companies owed motorists up to $38 million in New York and $300 million nationwide. Insurers blamed human error for the oversight, claiming that they relied on questions posed to drivers by the service representatives. New York's attorney general said insurers didn't try hard enough. They could have consulted the industry-sponsored Insurance Institute for Highway Safety, which publishes lists of cars with air bags and automatic belts. Or they could simply have programmed their computers to read a customer's vehicle identification number (VIN), which shows whether a car has air bags or automatic belts. Most of the accused insurers checked their records and said they planned to give retroactive discounts to eligible policyholders. One insurer, State Farm, said it would pay accrued interest as well.

If you think you may be owed a refund, your agent or insurer's customer service office should be able to help you. But don't be surprised if your insurer doesn't cooperate at first. A Consumers Union staffer called her insurance company about a discount for the air bag in her 1990 *Dodge Spirit*. She was told, "If you were supposed to get the discount, you got it." She then insisted that someone check her policy, and a supervisor found she was owed $28 a year for two years.

Pay All at Once

If you can afford it, pay the total premium up front—instead of by installments. This tactic may save you a few dollars in fees.

INSURING A RENTAL CAR

Countless drivers know the annoyance of being confronted at the rental-car counter by the question of buying extra insurance for their rental car. This quasi-insurance, known as the *collision-damage waiver* or *loss-damage waiver* (CDW/LDW), is one of the most expensive auto coverages offered. For a hefty fee, the car-rental company waives its right to hold you liable if the car is stolen or damaged.

To hear many rental agents tell it, saying no to CDW/LDW is as unwise as passing up a lifeboat leaving the *Titanic.* Agents have reason to push hard for the coverage, however—their employers profit handsomely from it. Whereas CDW/LDW costs motorists an extra $15 a day, industry sources say it costs the rental companies only about $1.50 per car, per day to provide.

In spite of warnings by car-rental agents, most people don't need CDW/LDW. If you're renting a car within the United States, it's quite likely that your auto insurance policy covers you and any drivers you designate to drive your rental car. If you pay for collision and comprehensive coverage on your own car, you will be covered up to the same

limits—and with the same deductibles—as on your own policy. If this is the case, you can merely reject CDW/LDW as an option when it is offered to you at the rental counter.

If you're going on a business trip, be sure to check before you rent to confirm that your personal policy includes car rentals for business purposes. While many insurance companies do supply this coverage, a growing number in several states have begun limiting their rental coverage to pleasure driving. Policyholders may have to buy an endorsement to extend their auto insurance to rental cars used for business. Alternatively, employees of large companies may be able to get coverage through their company's self-insurance or by a special arrangement between the employer and a particular rental company.

Your insurance policy may also limit the number of days it will insure a rental car for pleasure use. Government Employees Insurance Company (GEICO), for instance, limits coverage to 30 consecutive days; for more coverage, you'd have to return the car and then rerent it. State Farm limits personal use to 21 days, but if you have coverage for two cars on your auto insurance policy, that limit would jump to 42 days.

The Credit Card Option

If you're not covered by your auto insurance company (or if you don't ordinarily have auto insurance coverage), you may very well be covered by your credit card, especially if you own a premium or "gold" card. Owners of gold Visa, MasterCard, American Express, and Diners Club cards are automatically covered for collision or theft losses on rental cars so long as they use their charge cards to pay for the rental and decline the rental company's collision-damage or collision-loss waiver. Significantly, the credit cards cover rentals outside the United States, something standard auto insurance won't do.

Most credit-card coverage within the United States is secondary, however. This means that in the event of an accident or theft of the car, you would have to submit a claim first to your auto insurance carrier. The charge-card coverage doesn't release you from responsi-bility for any damage to the car, either. It merely promises to reimburse you for any payment that your auto insurer won't cover.

Beware of time limits. Gold Master-Card, for example, only covers rentals up to 15 days. Visa Gold provides 15-day coverage within the United States and 31-day coverage elsewhere. (Coverage by the standard cards, when available, varies by issuing bank.) American Express offers 31-day coverage world-wide. Diners Club offers 29 days of coverage, anywhere, for the full value of the rental car. If you must rent a car for longer periods, you may have to return and rerent it after the time limit has expired to extend your coverage.

HANDLING THE HARD SELL

Don't be intimidated by high-pressure sales pitches at the rental counter. Among the most common is a warning that the rental company doesn't have to deal with the charge-card company in the event you have an accident. In fact, the contract for coverage is between you and the charge-card company; the rental company's role is irrelevant.

Drivers may face an even tougher time abroad. In Europe and elsewhere, car-rental companies may refuse to rent cars without the collision-damage and loss-damage waivers (CDW/LDW). Some foreign car-rental companies have been accused of requiring consumers who decline CDW/LDW to hand over huge cash deposits, or put a "hold" on thousands of dollars on their credit cards against the possibility of an accident. The best defense against these kinds of scare tactics is to arrange for your car rental while still in the United States and indicate that you'll be relying on your charge card—not CDW/LDW—for your insurance coverage. It also probably pays to use a major multinational rental company that is accustomed to dealing with Americans who use credit cards for insurance coverage. If in spite of protests you're unable to rent a car abroad without buying CDW/LDW, note on the contract that you accepted the coverage under duress. When you return home, demand a full refund.

Some credit-card issuers have other limitations. American Express, for example, will offer collision coverage only for autos rented from the top 15 car rental companies. Check with your credit-card issuer to be sure the rental company you intend to use is eligible.

Be sure, too, to include on the rental agreement the name of anyone likely to drive the rental car. This addition can add an extra expense, but it also protects that driver under your credit-card coverage.

About the only people who must buy CDW/LDW are drivers who don't have collision and theft covered by their regular auto insurance or credit cards. If you're in this category, don't try to avoid obtaining CDW/LDW just to save a few dollars. Some coverage—even if it's prohibitively expensive—is better than none.

Rental Liability

A car-rental company is legally obligated to have liability insurance coverage for every car it owns. If your rental car damages another car, the car-rental company's insurance will pay the costs up to the limits of the policy. As long as bodily injury and car damage claims don't exceed those limits, you owe noth-

ing. Unfortunately, the 14 major car-rental companies in the United States cover their cars only to state liability minimums, which are generally very low (see pages 8–9). If the accident you caused incurs damage above those limits, you or your insurance company could be liable for the difference.

That's not a problem for most drivers, who are covered for liability on rental cars up to the limits on their regular auto policies. Again, it's wise to check your policy to make sure.

The only drivers who need to worry about rental liability insurance are those who don't drive at home and thus don't have auto liability insurance. If you're in this category, ask an insurance agent about buying temporary liability coverage. Or, if you must buy CDW/LDW, find out if it includes liability coverage. Some of these contracts do, which can save you a little money.

Note: Collision- or loss-damage waivers aren't legal in New York or Illinois. So if you rent your car in either state, you needn't worry about collision and theft coverage. The law in New York requires car-rental companies to cover physical damage to the automobile above the sum of $100; in Illinois, it's $200.

5

Filing a Claim

—

You're sitting in your car by the side of the road, in a near-panic. While you were waiting at a light, the driver behind you plowed into your back fender. Now you're facing the prospect of dealing with the police, the insurance company, the appraiser, and a body shop. You'll have to do without your car for a few days and, to top it off, you're late for an important appointment.

Take a deep breath and try to collect your thoughts. You'll need a clear head to answer questions from the police and to obtain the right information for your insurer.

WHAT TO DO IN AN ACCIDENT

What do you do if you have an automobile accident? The Insurance Information Institute, an industry-sponsored organization, recommends several steps to take in those first frantic moments

and hours after an accident. Its suggestions will help to expedite your claims.

1. Get help for anyone who is injured. Contact the police or highway patrol and explain briefly what happened, how many people are injured, and how badly they are hurt. The police can contact the ambulance or rescue squad more quickly than you can.
2. Don't try to move any injured persons; cover them with a blanket to keep them from getting cold and going into shock.
3. If your car is in the middle of the road and in danger of further damage, or if it will endanger someone else, put up flares or try to move it.
4. Cooperate fully with the police, and give them whatever information they require. To the institute's advice we add that you

should avoid any hasty admission of guilt in causing the accident. Even if you believe, in your upset state, that you did cause an accident, you may in fact *not* have done so. Be certain you tell the police only what you know are the facts. Do not report your assumptions, guesses, or beliefs as fact.

5. Find out from the police where you can obtain a copy of the police report. If you are unfamiliar with the area, it can be confusing to try to figure out what municipality you were in when the accident occurred.

6. Make sure you obtain the following information: the names and addresses of all drivers and passengers in the accident; the license plate numbers, makes, and models of all cars involved; and all drivers' license identification numbers and insurance identification numbers. If there are witnesses, make a note of their names and addresses, as well as the names of the responding police officers or other officials. Make a habit of carrying a pen and paper in your car at all times so they are handy if there's an accident.

7. If you have a camera, photograph the accident scene, including skid marks. If you don't have a camera, make a rough sketch of the scene.

8. If you run into an unattended car or object and you can't find the owner, leave your name, address, and telephone number.

9. Call your insurance agent or local representative as soon as possible. Carry the company's phone number with you so that you can contact your insurer promptly if you're away from home. Ask what forms or documents you will need to file your claim. This will probably include the police report and any auto repair and medical bills. An insurance company will probably want to have an insurance adjuster inspect your car and appraise the damage before you have the car repaired.

10. Cooperate with your insurer in its investigation, settlement, or defense of any claim, and turn over to the company copies of any legal papers you receive. If there is a lawsuit, and you have reported the accident promptly, your insurer will defend you.

11. Be sure to keep careful records of all your expenses, including lost wages, rental-car expenses, or the amounts you might have to pay a temporary housekeeper for services you can't perform due to accident-related injuries. Some insurance coverages will pay for these costs.

12. Keep copies of all paperwork. You may need to refer later to such papers.

When Should You File a Claim?

Many people wonder if they should report to their insurers those small accidents that involve only minor damage to their car, fearing that such a report could raise their insurance rates. That's a legitimate concern. Each claim you file can mean substantial surcharges if the company believes you were primarily at fault.

At Government Employees Insurance Company (GEICO) and its subsidiary, GEICO General Insurance Company, even one reported at-fault accident could remove you from the lowest-premium category. State Farm's two subsidiaries add a 10 to 50 percent surcharge to the total premium for three years for each at-fault ("chargeable") accident that costs the company more than $400; surcharges at Nationwide's subsidiaries range from 30 to 70 percent for three years. In fact, some companies—and some states—require surcharges for speeding tickets and other moving violations.

Most states forbid insurers to cancel a policy before its expiration date unless policyholders fail to pay the premium or, for whatever reason, lose their license. Insurers can opt not to renew a policy when it expires, however. Too many claims—say, three in a three-year period—will threaten your coverage. It doesn't matter if the claims are only for a few hundred dollars each; insurers are concerned about the frequency as much as the dollar amount.

So when should you report an accident? Always, insurers say, because if they find out about any accident you didn't report, you could be dropped for breach of contract. Certainly, if there's a lot of damage and another car and passengers are involved, it's always appropriate to report an accident.

On the other hand, if you have had a claim recently and the new damage isn't much above the deductible, you may choose not to report it. Many people don't report such accidents but settle with the other driver and pay their own repair bills out of pocket to avoid penalties.

This strategy could backfire, though, if the other driver later files a claim with your company. Your insurer could then drop you, or refuse to defend you in a lawsuit, for failing to report the accident. What is more, some state laws say motorists must report accidents where the property damage was greater than a certain amount, perhaps $500. If motorists do not and are caught, they could face the maximum penalty: jail.

Filing with the Other Insurer

If the other driver was clearly at fault in an accident that damaged property only, you can file a claim with his or her insurance company instead of with your own. This strategy has one chief advantage: You don't have to pay your deductible up front.

If you choose to follow this route, be aware that the entire process may take longer. The other company may feel no

---

THE GLASS FACTOR

A vandal smashes in one of the side windows of your car as it sits parked on a city street. Your son hits a baseball right through the rear window of your new car. Congratulations—you're now a statistic. About half of all comprehensive (noncollision) claims involve glass damage.

Repairing a smashed window may seem like a minor expense but, in fact, the cost can be considerable. A windshield on a late-model car can cost more than $1,000 to replace.

To reduce these expenses, several insurers now offer a special deal to their policyholders: If the glass is repaired instead of replaced, they will waive the glass deductible. For the average driver, that's a savings of $100.

United Services Automobile Association (USAA) is one insurer with such a program. However, the damage must be in a place that doesn't interfere with the driver's vision. A clear compound is used to make the repair, and it usually guarantees that a crack in the glass won't expand. If the damage does spread, USAA promises to pay for a complete window replacement at no charge to the driver.

---

pressure to satisfy someone who isn't its customer.

In our survey of insurance companies (see Appendix A), readers who filed with the other driver's insurer found their payments delayed by more than 30 days at least 43 percent of the time. For those dealing with their own insurance companies, payments were delayed only 9 percent of the time.

Choosing a Body Shop

Many car owners choose a body shop recommended by their insurer. Larger insurers often maintain relationships with hundreds of body shops in a region, so you're likely to find one on the company's list that suits you. Moreover, if you bring your car to an insurer-designated shop, the company often requires the shop to guarantee the repairs for a given period. The established relationship between the insurer and the repair shop also could mean fewer problems with estimates and repair quality.

But don't take your insurer's advice without investigating other options. Talk to friends and acquaintances, and seek recommendations. Ask the adjuster or appraiser as well. Though state laws sometimes prohibit them from steering customers to a certain body shop, they may be allowed to recommend one when asked. At the least, they may be able to tell you which local shops to avoid. Some car owners get several independent estimates before settling on any one body shop. Be aware, however, that the insurer may not pay the cost, if any, of extra estimates.

According to the American Automobile Association, it's a good idea to work with a body shop certified by the National Institute for Automotive Service Excellence. Check also with the local Better Business Bureau or state division of consumer affairs to find out whether the shop has a record of complaints and violations.

If your car was towed to a repair shop, you don't have to keep it there. If you move it, however, you may have to pay out of your own pocket for the first shop's estimate and storage. Check with your insurer for its specific rules relating to these charges.

The Appraisal Process

Unless the damage to your car is minor, your insurer will probably send an appraiser or adjuster to inspect your car for damage. An adjuster often has the authority to write a check directly to you after the inspection. Appraisers, who are trained in auto mechanics, can assess the value of damages but usually must report their results to an adjuster at the company. The adjuster then authorizes a check.

Appraisers and adjusters will come to your house, to your office parking lot, or to a garage—wherever it's convenient for you—to check out the car. Your responsibility is to make the car available; some states require compliance within a certain time period. It's often an advantage to have the car in a commercial garage so the appraiser can use a lift to look underneath for unnoticed damage.

The appraisal can take between five minutes to half an hour, depending on the damage.

To accommodate policyholders, larger insurers often operate drive-in appraisal centers. Inspectors print out the appraisal on the spot, transmit their results to an off-site adjuster, and usually are able to write a check for the customer within a short time.

Some larger insurers don't require an appraisal at all if motorists agree to take their car to a designated body shop. Assuming the driver gives permission, the shop appraises the car and begins work immediately. Occasionally, the shop may lend you a car while yours is being fixed, even if you don't have insurance to pay for a rental car in such situations.

If you're present during the appraisal, be sure to point out any special features of the car, such as customized paint details, that the appraiser may have overlooked. You or the body shop may be able to negotiate a higher settlement with the insurer in that case.

If the car is already in a body shop before the appraisal, *don't authorize any repairs until it's inspected.* Only the adjuster can say what the insurer will pay for and what it won't cover. Usually, you don't need to be involved directly in negotiations; the adjuster and the body shop manager will work out the settlement. If the body shop workers find other problems later, they will contact the insurer and arrange for additional payment. If the body shop communicates early with the insurer, you probably won't have to put down any money in advance. Some shops may require you to pay your deductible up front, however.

Even though you may not be involved in cost negotiations, be sure to get a copy of the estimate. Note whether any of the repair parts are used parts or parts made by manufacturers other than the car manufacturer (they're often called "aftermarket" parts). These types of parts are used most often to replace the outer "skin" of the car: doors, hood, and roof, for instance. Insurers prefer these parts because they're often less expensive than parts by the original manufacturer. In many cases, these parts are just as good as the original ones, but if you have doubts, ask the body shop for an objective assessment. In some cases, it may be better to use new or original equipment, but be warned that your insurer doesn't have to pay the extra cost. Its legal responsibility is to make the car look and run as it did before the accident, not to make the car like new. So, if it's a seven-year-old car, it may very well get a seven-year-old replacement bumper.

Handling Abuses. According to a 1992 *Consumer Reports* survey report, promptness in claims handling is the single most significant factor in whether or not a consumer is satisfied with insurance service. It's no surprise, then, that some companies make a policy of settling claims as quickly as possible. In addition, many states have regulations concerning unfair-claims practices; these establish minimum standards and definitions of deceptive practices by insurers. If you believe your company may be taking too long on your claim, report it to your state insurance department. Be aware, however, that the company probably won't be punished unless it has a record of such abuses.

Furthermore, reporting an abuse doesn't help much if you're still waiting for a claim to be settled so you can get your car fixed. Your best remedy is preventive: Choose a company that has a good record for settling claims (see Appendix A). According to the *Consumer Reports* survey, 48 percent of respondents received a total payment from their insurer within seven days of reporting the claim. Another 27 percent received payment between 7 and 14 days after filing, and only 9 percent had to wait more than 30 days.

MEDICAL CLAIMS

A fender bender can leave you shaken up, but it doesn't compare with the trauma of suffering an actual injury from a car accident. One out of six car accidents results in bodily injury to a driver, passenger, or pedestrian. For those unlucky people, it's hard enough enduring discomfort, pain, or loss without worrying about dealing with the insurance company and possibly waiting years for a complete settlement.

Fortunately, many drivers are able to settle with their own or another driver's

WHEN YOUR CAR IS A TOTAL LOSS

When a car is stolen or its repair cost approaches or exceeds its actual cash value or market value, the insurer may declare it a total loss. Most likely, the insurer will pay you the market price of your car, minus the deductible, and base that price on the assumption your car was in only average condition. If you disagree and think your car was in better-than-average shape, submit copies of written service records or a mechanic's statement to the insurance company. You may get more money for it.

Unfortunately, if you have an outstanding car loan for more than the car's current value, you may end up with no car and a loan still to pay off. One solution, called *exchange of collateral,* is sometimes used by larger insurers, such as State Farm and Allstate, and by large lenders, such as General Motors Acceptance Corporation (GMAC). Let's say you have a $15,000 car loan financed by GMAC, but State Farm, your insurer, is willing to pay out only $11,000. State Farm may agree to take title to your car and, with your and GMAC's approval, find you another car valued at $11,000. You're still responsible for the $15,000 loan, but at least you have a car.

Recently, a few insurers have begun offering "gap" insurance to buyers of new cars. The insurance, usually sold through the auto dealer, covers the remaining costs of your auto loan that are not paid by your standard auto insurance if a new car is totaled or stolen. A driver covered by such a policy gets a new replacement car, and the dealer is paid the difference between the claim settlement and the cost of the replacement car. One insurer, for example, offers such coverage in California but charges about $350 for two years for an average-price new car. At that price, "gap" insurance appears to be a very expensive coverage that does more to protect the dealer than the car owner.

insurance company within a few days or weeks of the accident. And more than 90 percent of claims involving bodily injury are settled before they reach a courtroom. Getting your due may not be as daunting if you are aware of the procedures involved.

No-Fault States

In states with no-fault insurance, your and your family's injuries are covered under personal-injury protection coverage, or PIP. You are covered up to the limits prescribed in your policy.

Generally, the PIP portion of your auto insurance policy is the primary source of coverage in the event you're hurt in an accident, followed by any medical payments coverage that you've purchased. (Unlike health insurance, "med pay" carries no deductible.) Once you've exhausted those sources, your health insurance or disability coverage may pay what's left over. Every carrier has different rules, however, so check your health insurance policy carefully.

If you live in a no-fault state (see box below), the processing for filing a bodily injury claim is essentially the same as for filing a property damage claim. After you report the accident to your insurer, the company will assign an adjuster to handle your medical claim. First, the adjuster must determine whether the injuries are covered under the policy.

Don't be surprised if the adjuster also asks probing questions about your health and employment prior to the accident. The adjuster is trying to figure out if a bad knee, for example, is a result of the reported accident or if it's a problem you've had for years. Similarly, if you assert you can't work because of the injuries, the adjuster will want to make sure you weren't already unemployed before the accident.

Many no-fault policies pay a portion of lost wages and the cost of services, such as child care, incurred as a result of the accident. So it is important to record these costs as they arise.

As you incur medical bills, submit them to the insurer. In most states, insurers aren't permitted to tell you where to seek medical help or what kind of help to get. (One insurance official complained that some customers even submit bills for trips to Lourdes, France, a traditional site of healing.) However, insurers may intervene in your medical treatment to control costs. Often, that involves assigning a rehabilitation nurse with experience in accident-related injuries to follow your case and suggest treatments the insurer considers cost-effective.

Colorado has attempted to legally mandate cost controls. For a 20-percent reduction in the PIP premium, drivers can agree to go to a medical provider (generally an HMO or similar facility) recommended by the auto insurance carrier.

Settling Disputes

Insurers in no-fault states may refuse to pay for costs they feel are not "customary and reasonable" for treating your injuries, especially in a particular

---

IS YOUR STATE A NO-FAULT STATE?

Currently, 13 states and Puerto Rico have no-fault auto insurance laws in effect with restrictions on filing suit. Florida, Michigan, New Jersey, New York, and Pennsylvania have *verbal thresholds,* which means you may sue for pain and suffering only if your injuries or losses fit into the categories as stated by law. Colorado, Hawaii, Kansas, Kentucky, Massachusetts, Minnesota, North Dakota, and Utah have *monetary thresholds,* which means that people with injuries can sue for pain and suffering only when the cost of treating those injuries exceeds a dollar amount set by law.

region or area. The company, though, must furnish a good reason for refusing payment (probably the most disputed treatment is repeated chiropractic visits). If you feel your claim has been unfairly rejected, contact the consumer affairs division of your state's insurance department (see Appendix B). Although the state probably can't change the insurer's decision, officials may be able to give you a clearer explanation of why the insurer rejected your claim. Or you may want to seek the advice of an attorney.

In disputes involving large sums of money, it probably will be necessary to get a lawyer's assistance. You stand a better chance of having your bills paid if you or the lawyer can show that the wording of the insurance policy is vague and ambiguous. Courts generally rule in favor of policyholders in such cases.

What can you do if your medical bills exceed your coverage in a no-fault state? Health or disability insurance, if you have it, may fill in the gaps. If you believe you were not at fault and have experienced unnecessary pain and suffering, you could sue the other driver to collect more damages. However, the rules on when and if you can sue vary from state to state. In some states, your medical bills must exceed a certain dollar amount, known as a *monetary* or *dollar threshold*. In others, you must prove that

THE UNINSURED DRIVER

According to the California Department of Motor Vehicles, nearly a quarter of all California drivers are uninsured; that is, they have no auto liability insurance. In other states uninsured drivers are fewer, but they're still common in many urban areas. If you drive in a city or its environs anywhere in the United States, you stand a greater chance than in other areas of being struck by a driver who is underinsured—that is, carrying only the bare state minimums—or by a driver who is completely uninsured.

Many drivers have uninsured and underinsured motorist coverage included in their policies; some no-fault states require it. In the event you are injured—either as a driver or a pedestrian—by an uninsured motorist, you can then file a claim with your own company. Your claim is treated as if the uninsured motorist were the company's client instead of you. This means you may have to go through the same negotiation process with your insurer as if you were the outside aggrieved party. If a dispute arises concerning payment, you may have to call in an attorney, and you may face the uncomfortable prospect of going to court against your own insurer.

Fortunately, some states have laws to speed up settlements between a motorist and his insurer in an uninsured/underinsured claim dispute. Illinois and Rhode Island, for instance, allow for arbitration in such cases. In fact, the majority of disputes are settled by arbitration, which reduces costs and results in a quicker resolution of the case.

the injury is chronic or severe, or involves broken bones or loss of use of a body part or organ, among other requirements. That's called a *verbal threshold,* because the conditions for filing the lawsuit are described by words, not by monetary limits.

States Without No-Fault

In states without no-fault laws, people who are injured in an auto accident must rely on the other driver's insurer to pay their medical costs. How much they are reimbursed depends on the circumstances of the accident, the severity of the injuries, the cost of medical treatment, and the other driver's coverage.

The claims procedure is nearly identical to that in a no-fault state. Following an accident, as soon as you are able to do so, you'll need to call your own insurer. Supply vital details, including the other driver's license and registration numbers, and the name of his or her insurance company. Then contact the other driver's insurer to file a claim. As with no-fault claims, that insurer will assign an adjuster to interview you.

The other driver's insurer will go through a series of steps to determine what, if anything, it is willing to pay you for your injuries. First, it evaluates whether your injuries are covered by its customer's policy. Next, it looks at who was at fault. Depending on state laws, proof that you were partly negligent in the accident could keep you from getting any settlement at all.

Negligence: Who's at Fault?

Negligence is the failure of a person to exercise as much care in his or her ac-

---

ASSESSING THE DAMAGE

How do adjusters determine damages in a bodily injury case? To hear the insurance companies tell it, it's a mysterious art, with no easily explained system. They do admit, however, that several factors are taken into account when arriving at an award figure. Foremost are the current and projected medical costs, called *special damages,* or "specials." Once these costs are established, insurers consider the type and duration of the medical treatment involved, the severity of the injured party's pain and suffering, the length of the recovery period, and the seriousness and permanence of the injury.

Other considerations enter into the insurer's calculations, including the individual's occupation. A pianist whose hand is damaged might be offered much more than, say, a librarian with a similar injury. Health records are important: Diabetics, for example, might take longer to recover than others.

tions as a reasonably prudent person would be expected to do in the same circumstances. For accidents involving two parties, three main types of negligence laws exist in the United States: *pure comparative negligence, modified comparative negligence, and contributory negligence.* To understand how these concepts work, consider the hypothetical case of driver A, who is driving slightly above the speed limit and is struck at an intersection by driver B, who turned the corner without signaling. Let's assume that, if this case went to trial, driver A would be judged 30 percent at fault; driver B, on the other hand, is 70 percent at fault. The cost of injuries and property damage for each driver is estimated at $10,000.

In the 13 states that operate under *pure comparative negligence* (see following box), damages are awarded that reflect how the portion of blame is attributed to each driver in an accident. In this case, driver A, who was judged 30 percent at fault, would be entitled to collect $7,000, or 70 percent of his estimated damages, from driver B's insurer. Driver B, who was judged 70 percent at fault, would collect $3,000, or 30 percent, from driver A's carrier.

In the 32 states with *modified comparative negligence,* only the driver considered less at fault could collect. In our example, driver A would collect the same amount—$7,000—but driver B would get nothing. There are two variations of this law, however. In 12 states, drivers cannot collect even part of the

damages unless their share of the negligence is 49 percent or less. In 20 other states, drivers can collect if their share is 50 percent or less. (When the share of blame is fifty-fifty, both parties collect.) South Dakota, however, requires that drivers prove that their negligence was minor in order to receive any portion of the damages.

Four states and the District of Columbia use the doctrine of *contributory negligence:* Drivers are paid no damages if they are found to be even 1 percent at fault.

The other driver's insurer will also insist on evidence of your damages: medical bills, proof of loss of income, and so forth. As you incur medical bills over time, send them to an adjuster or to an attorney you've chosen to represent you.

Once your doctors are certain about the severity and duration of your injuries, and assuming your account of the accident corresponds generally to that of witnesses and the other driver, the insurer's adjuster and your attorney will attempt to negotiate a lump-sum settlement to cover your current and future costs, or damages.

Those damages are intended to compensate you not only for your medical expenses but also for any pain and suffering, lost wages, and opportunities missed because of your injuries. The adjuster's job is to restore you financially to where you were before the accident. In some states, you also can be awarded punitive damages if the other driver is found to have been reckless.

STATE NEGLIGENCE LAWS

PURE (COMPARATIVE)

Alaska
Arizona
California
Florida
Kentucky
Louisiana
Michigan
Mississippi
Missouri
New Mexico
New York
Rhode Island
Washington

MODIFIED (49% NEGLIGENCE OR LESS)

Arkansas
Colorado
Georgia
Idaho
Kansas
Maine
Nebraska
North Dakota
Tennessee
Utah
West Virginia
Wyoming

MODIFIED (50% NEGLIGENCE OR LESS)

Connecticut
Delaware
Hawaii
Illinois
Indiana
Iowa
Massachusetts
Minnesota
Montana
Nevada
New Hampshire
New Jersey
Ohio
Oklahoma
Oregon
Pennsylvania
South Carolina
Texas
Vermont
Wisconsin

CONTRIBUTORY

Alabama
District of Columbia
Maryland
North Carolina
Virginia

UNIQUE

South Dakota

Source: Alliance of American Insurers

LITIGATION: TO SUE OR NOT TO SUE

Should you use a lawyer? If you dislike the negotiation process, it may be a good idea to contact an attorney. It's also wise to find a lawyer if your injuries are severe or appear to be long-term or permanently disabling.

If the insurer refuses to pay, you may have no other choice but to hire an attorney to pursue the claim. You may introduce a lawyer to the process at any time during the claims or negotiations procedures, up to the time you cash the settlement check. (Most states have statutes of limitations on how long one can wait to sue for pain and suffering.) Once you have legal help, however, you may only communicate with the insurance company through your attorney.

There are several advantages to having an experienced negotiator on your side. An important one is the perception that you'll get a bigger settlement if you are represented by a lawyer. Insurers, of course, claim that they offer the same amount of damages whether or not an attorney is involved. However, studies show that attorneys may help a typical driver retrieve about 10 percent more in an auto injury case than the driver could receive by negotiating without a lawyer. Indeed, according to one study conducted by Rand's Institute for Civil Justice, people with lesser injuries get a greater return from using attorneys than do people with more serious cases who do not use a lawyer.

In the end, however, all these extra costs come back to haunt drivers, because they're reflected in higher insurance premiums. For this reason, many consumer advocates favor a no-fault system, which, by limiting lawsuits, discourages inflation of claims and more fairly compensates seriously injured people.

Having an attorney, of course, can also take a bite out of your settlement. A lawyer's fees can eat up 30 to 40 percent of a settlement. And that doesn't include costs incurred if the case goes to trial, such as for special witnesses and depositions. These expenses directly affect what you'll pocket in the end and, in a larger sense, add on to the cost of insurance in general.

Lawsuits can be difficult, emotionally draining experiences. The wait to trial also can be lengthy. The average auto injury case takes about 37 months from the filing of the claim to the awarding of the settlement. In the meantime, your medical bills (and your blood pressure) may be mounting.

Fortunately, only about 10 percent of personal-injury cases go to trial. The rest are settled out of court, in formal or informal negotiations. You or your attorney can either negotiate directly with the insurer or employ one of several forms of *alternative dispute resolution* to come up with a final settlement. This form of negotiation, which uses a trained, neutral third party, often precludes the need to go to trial.

Several types of alternative dispute

resolution mechanisms are in use. In *binding arbitration,* a paid, independent arbitrator—often a lawyer or retired judge—works out a settlement with the agreement of both parties. *Nonbinding arbitration* works the same way, although you're not required to accept the outcome. In *mediation,* a third party is paid to work between both litigants but then leaves the final settlement up to them.

Keep Good Records. Regardless of the severity of the accident, the most important single thing you can do is to keep good, accurate records. Maintain a separate file on your accident claim or claims. Make copies of everything; when the insurance company requests documents, send the copies. Take detailed notes, including times and dates, of con-versations with insurance company representatives, lawyers, and the police. The more information you have at your fingertips, the more easily and quickly your claim will be resolved.

If the Other Driver Sues. At the same time you're considering your options, the other driver may also take action. What do you do if he or she sues your insurance company?

For the most part, you don't have to be involved in your company's negotiations with the other driver. However, every insurance policy contains a clause that states your obligations in the matter. For example, you must agree to provide statements, when requested, concerning the accident. You may also be asked to provide documents and, if the case goes to court, to appear and testify.

6

Insurance Pitfalls

—

As discussed previously, you can save a significant amount of money by comparison shopping for auto insurance. Not only do some insurance companies offer lower premiums than others, but any two companies can come to far different conclusions about the degree of risk presented by the same applicants.

Increasingly, though, carriers faced with declining profits from auto insurance have tightened their underwriting standards. Claiming they can't make money on the regulated rates that states allow them to charge, these companies are offering policies to only the best drivers—that is, to those with the most unblemished driving records. Obviously, this type of selection leaves quite a few motorists—the so-called high-risk drivers—without coverage.

Drivers who can't find an insurer to voluntarily cover them end up in the shared insurance market, or the *high-*

risk plan. Coverage is guaranteed—for a price.

THE HIGH-RISK PLAN

Many of us know some unlucky person who, for one reason or another, has been placed in a state high-risk insurance plan, or pool. This institution serves an important function: insuring drivers who can't find a private or "voluntary" insurer to cover them. The high-risk category usually entails higher auto insurance rates, sometimes several times higher than the amount motorists would pay in the private market. And while many eventually are able to escape the high-risk pool and return to the private market, many good drivers linger in this insurance limbo indefinitely.

The drivers that high-risk insurance is meant to cover are (1) those who have been convicted of many moving violations or (2) those who have caused so many accidents that no private insurer wants them. Accident-prone drivers pay more because the damage they have caused—and are projected to cause—will cost the insurers too much money.

Nevertheless, millions of drivers with no record of accidents also end up in the high-risk category. In fact, according to the National Insurance Consumers Organization, 60 to 80 percent of all drivers in state-sponsored auto insurance plans have had no accidents or traffic tickets in the previous three years.

Although state laws often stipulate that insurers are not to look beyond three years of a driver's record, agents sometimes ask particular applicants for a five-year driving history. Such scrutiny can hurt many drivers' chances of getting covered.

Who are the vulnerable drivers? For one, young or new drivers run the risk of falling into the high-risk category. Young drivers are statistically more likely to be involved in accidents, and many auto insurers don't like to take a gamble on drivers who have less than three years' driving experience.

Drivers who are new to the United States—even those with years of accident-free driving elsewhere—also may be initially rejected by private insurers. Again, companies claim that they need at least three years of local driving data to accurately project a driver's possible future accident record and, hence, the driver's premiums. Some drivers may even be rejected by regular insurers because their mastery of English is insufficient.

Divorced people, too, have landed in the high-risk category. If their financial situation after divorce changes for the worse, they may be judged poor risks. Also, insurers consider unmarried drivers to be poorer risks than married ones. And if you've never caused an accident but have been the victim of several in a relatively short period of time, a regular insurer may refuse to accept you. Your only choice may be the state high-risk plan.

People from marginal or poor neighborhoods often end up in the high-risk plan, even if they have spotless driving records. Companies don't want to insure a car that's kept where it's more likely to be vandalized or stolen. Even if low-income drivers don't buy coverage for theft or physical damage, they may find it difficult to obtain even the minimum state-required liability coverage from a private insurer, simply because few insurers have offices or representatives in poorer neighborhoods.

Indeed, some consumer activists say insurers "redline" poor urban neighborhoods by refusing to locate offices or work with agencies in those areas. A report in 1992 by the New York State Department of Consumer Affairs noted that nearly half of New York City drivers were covered by the state's assigned-risk plan, compared with less than 14 percent in the rest of the state. In poor areas such as the South Bronx, 82 percent of motorists were covered by the plan. The state suggested in its report that insurers consciously discourage agents from setting up agencies or writing policies in those areas. Insurers countered that there is no conscious redlining; their offices are placed where they believe they can make money.

How High-Risk Plans Work

Every state sponsors some form of insurance for high-risk drivers, who are known in the business as the *residual market*. Even if you're not in your state's high-risk plan, you're probably subsidizing it through the premiums you pay to your regular carrier.

In most states, the residual market is covered by the *assigned-risk plan,* so named because an insurer that does business in a state is assigned to cover a certain percentage of high-risk drivers. The number of drivers each insurer covers in the assigned-risk pool corresponds to the percentage of drivers the company covers in the private market. Thus, an insurer with many auto insurance customers in a given state has to cover many more high-risk drivers than a company with fewer customers. When an insurer loses money from its high-risk drivers—as often happens—it then charges all its customers higher premiums to make up its loss.

In a few states, the residual market is handled by a state-run *joint underwriting association,* or JUA. With a JUA, a few companies agree, for a fee, to service the policies of all the state's high-risk drivers. These so-called servicing carriers deal with JUA-insured drivers just as they would with their regular customers, but they assume no financial responsibilities for JUA insurance policies. If the JUA loses money, the state may surcharge JUA-insured drivers, or all policyholders in the state, to cover that loss.

Reinsurance facilities also have been established in some states. A reinsurance facility is a nonprofit entity. Unlike other systems that insure high-risk drivers, insurers in states with reinsurance facilities are required to accept all applicants but are permitted to cede a percentage of drivers—usually the highest risks—to the reinsurance pool. The reinsurance facility is the official insurer, but the private companies collect the premiums and service the policies. If the facility loses money, it requires all auto insurers in the state to share the loss. Those losses get passed on to all drivers indirectly in higher premiums.

One state—Maryland—is unique in that it has a state-owned insurance company called the Maryland Auto Insurance Fund. To be eligible for the fund, a driver must have been rejected by two private carriers. The fund pays for its losses by charging an annual assessment to all auto insurers in the state. Companies are then allowed to periodically assess all policyholders, not just high-risk drivers, to make up the difference.

High-risk coverage is bought in the same way as regular coverage: through an agent, broker, or telephone customer service representative. In fact, a high-risk policy may carry the same company logo as a regular policy. It's only when you look closely that you see "assigned risk" or some other words that indicate the state's sponsorship. In most states, the insurer services an assigned-risk policy—that is, it collects the premiums, pays claims, handles complaints—the same way it services its own customers.

How Good Drivers Can Avoid the Assigned-Risk Plan

Many good drivers end up in assigned-risk plans for reasons that may seem incomprehensible to the average person. Again, consider the plight of someone who's returning to the United States after many years in another country. That person may have had a perfect driving record abroad, but American companies don't want to take the gamble of insuring someone with no recent claims experience. The same can be said for immigrants, only more so.

If that is your situation, you may be able to persuade an insurer to immediately place you in its standard subsidiary if you can produce good driving and claims records from your previous country of residence. Try to have those documents ready, or send for them in advance of applying for coverage. Placing both your auto and homeowner's coverage with a single company can also make a difference.

Teenagers make up a large part of the assigned-risk population. Private insurers may be more inclined to insure them, however, if they're included on a parent's policy. Some insurers will charge the highest rate to the car driven by the teenager, whereas others assume the teenager will sometimes drive other cars listed on the policy. In that case, they will charge the teenager's high rate to the most expensive car in the family. Usually, however, the family will still save more money with a single policy than if the teenager were covered under a separate policy. (Some parents believe they will limit their own liability if teenagers have their own policy. That is not true. As long as teens still live with their parents, the parents can be held liable above the limits of the teens' policy.)

Once children are living on their own, they are required to have their own policies. College students are the exception. They are still considered members of their parents' household even if they live away from home. As mentioned before, families with students who reside at a college more than 100 miles from home can often obtain discounts from private insurers.

Getting out of the High-Risk Plan

The high-risk plan is expensive. An assigned-risk policy can cost many times more than an identical policy from the private market. That's because premiums are affected by the driving patterns of all the bad drivers in the pool. The state also may impose higher accident surcharges on assigned-risk drivers for moving violations and other infractions. As in a regular policy, those surcharges are included in the premium for as long as three years.

Assigned-risk policies often restrict the coverage you may buy, too. For example, you may not be allowed to buy collision or comprehensive coverage for your car. Or, you may be restricted to collision and comprehensive deductibles as high as $2,000. And you probably won't be entitled to any special discounts (see chapter 4).

Once you're in a high-risk plan, it may take years of proving yourself before you're eligible for lower premiums with a private company. Typically, you'd need three years of no accidents or violations to qualify for a standard insurance policy with a regular company. And some major insurers have been known to completely reject any motorist who has ever been in the high-risk category.

Several states have responded to the high-risk conundrum: They require insurers to accept *all* good drivers. If you are such a driver living in California, Hawaii, Massachusetts, Michigan, New Jersey, North Carolina, or South Carolina, you are entitled to buy insurance from the carrier of your choice. In most states, your record must show three years of no at-fault accidents. Remember, however, that a perfect driving record may not guarantee a company's best rate right away. Some insurers require drivers to be with them for several years, claim-free, before they are eligible for the lowest available premiums.

Pennsylvania offers another option to assigned-risk drivers who have had a clean driving record for three years or more. In that state, once a motorist has been in the assigned-risk plan for a year, the private company that provides the policy is required to offer the driver regular coverage. Unfortunately, the initial premium can be higher than the cost of the coverage the driver was paying in the assigned-risk plan. Insurance agents, however, often recommend that drivers accept this rare offer as the first step to entering, or reentering, the mainstream of auto insurance.

Avoiding the high-risk plan in the first place is the best strategy for paying lower premiums. Most important, drive safely to avoid moving violations and at-fault accidents. You're most likely to be accepted by a private insurer if you're accident-free.

It's also crucial to pay the premium on time. States often prohibit insurers from canceling customers for so-called trivial reasons, but nonpayment of the premium is not considered trivial. To avoid problems, it's probably a good idea to pay a week early. At the very least, make sure the agent or customer service department has received your premium payment the day before it's due. Insurers can legally count a payment for coverage late if it's not in their hands at 12:01 A.M. on the day the coverage is to begin.

NONRENEWAL OF POLICY

In most states, an insurer cannot unilaterally cancel a policy that has been in force more than 60 days unless it has very good reasons. Those reasons include:

- The premium was not paid on time.
- The driver's license, or the license of another driver who regularly uses the insured auto, has been suspended.
- The driver obtained coverage through fraud or misrepresentation. This stipulation can mean anything from lying about where the car is garaged to underreporting the mileage traveled to work.

Commonly, insurance companies try to get rid of customers by not offering to renew their coverage. For some insurers, two at-fault accidents could be considered cause for nonrenewal. It doesn't matter if the claims are only for a few hundred dollars each; insurers are concerned about the frequency of accidents as much as the dollar amount.

Insurers generally are more lenient toward claims on the comprehensive portion of an insurance policy. Comprehensive coverage protects against damage caused by something other than a collision (see chapter 2). But some carriers admit they probably would not renew the policy of an accident-prone customer.

The Ratings listed in Appendix A include the drop rates for 49 companies in a 1992 *Consumer Reports* survey report. The *drop rate* is defined as the percentage of survey respondents who were canceled or not renewed by a given company. It's a good guide to which companies are most lenient and which are the strictest. The most common reason for being dropped, according to the respondents, included too many claims, followed by too many traffic-law violations.

Shopping Around After Nonrenewal or Cancellation

If your company decides not to renew your policy, it must give you advance notice. Depending on the state where you reside, notice could be as few as 15 days or as many as 60. In any case, you should have time to shop around for a replacement policy. Indeed, it's important to start looking for a carrier immediately; if your case is difficult, it could take you or your agent or broker the full warning period to find adequate coverage for you.

For one thing, every prospective insurer will want to know as much as possible about you. So it's most important to be up front about your accident or claims history. If you don't mention something that later shows up in your CLUE report (see page 37), the insurer will surely be suspicious. Again, the key is proving to the agent or company representative that you have a stable work and living situation, and will be able to pay the premium on time.

After a few weeks of shopping, you may find that the best alternative outside the high-risk plan is a nonstandard company—that is, an insurer that offers coverage to higher-risk customers. Sometimes the company is an individual insurer that specializes in nonstandard policies. Or the insurer may be a subsidiary of a larger company that also has one or two less-expensive subsidiaries for drivers it considers less risky.

The coverage offered by the nonstandard company can, in some cases, be more expensive than what is offered in the state high-risk or assigned-risk plan. It still may be worth your while to buy the nonstandard coverage from the private company, however, because you may be able to move more quickly to the less-expensive subsidiaries. It's a calculated risk that may be to your advantage, but only when the price differential between the assigned-risk and nonstandard companies isn't that great.

7

Consumer Initiatives

—

In 1988, auto insurance was a main topic of conversation at almost every California dinner party or social gathering. Rural or urban, young or old, drivers in the state were angry at the high prices they had to pay for the privilege of driving a car. Across the country, in New Jersey, the mood was the same. One January day, hundreds of motorists jammed the streets of Trenton, the state capital, shouting slogans and holding banners. They made their feelings known about paying the highest average auto insurance premiums in the nation—nearly $1,000 annually per car.

Motorists all over the country were angry. In Arizona, Georgia, Michigan, Pennsylvania, Texas, and numerous other states, bills and voter initiatives for lowering auto insurance rates clogged legislatures. Insuring the family car had become an unbearable burden for the middle class and for the poor. Unfortunately, times have not changed all that much—in 1993 many Americans pay hundreds or even thousands of dollars a year for auto insurance.

TRYING TO CHANGE THE SYSTEM

Auto insurance is mandatory in nearly all states for anyone who drives. It's a regressive "tax," which means the poor and middle class pay as much as, or more than, the rich for the same coverage. A recent study by the California Department of Insurance shows that lower-income consumers in Los Angeles pay as much as 10 times as high a percentage of household income on auto insurance as affluent drivers do.

It's no wonder an estimated 20 percent of motorists nationwide drive illegally, without insurance, according to the National Insurance Consumer Organization. If these uninsured drivers are involved in an accident, they can sue the other driver. But if the other driver is injured, he or she can't recover anything from the uninsured driver unless uninsured motorist coverage was purchased (see chapter 2). Such irresponsibility on the part of some drivers results in higher premiums for all drivers. In California, where uninsured drivers make up one-quarter of all motorists, premiums for uninsured and underinsured-motorist coverage constitute a significant portion of each resident's total insurance premium.

Still, controversy exists on every aspect of auto insurance. Many say it's unfair to make people buy something they can't afford; others argue that the system in general is so unfair and costly that it hurts everyone. As a result, state legislatures around the nation have tried to address the current auto insurance situation through reform measures. Some of these laws appear to work; others have faltered or failed entirely.

Legislative Changes

In New Jersey a 1988 law erased a mandatory insurance surcharge of up to $222 on most cars in the state. This surcharge had subsidized the state-run joint underwriting association for high-risk drivers. Under a new law, drivers with a clean driving record were offered a reduction in premiums, whereas drivers with violations were forced to pay even higher rates than before. And for the first time, New Jersey motorists were given a choice between traditional tort liability insurance (which allows you to sue more freely for pain and suffering) and cheaper no-fault insurance.

In 1990 a Pennsylvania law also rolled back rates and capped the amount of medical costs that auto insurance would cover. It also offered consumers a significant number of money-saving choices, including the option of buying no-fault instead of tort liability coverage. One choice allows motorists with more than one car to buy uninsured and underinsured motorist coverage once for both cars, rather than duplicating each coverage at a slightly higher expense. According to Pennsylvania's insurance department, the total initiative saved motorists $1.4 billion in its first 18 months of implementation. In that period, average annual premiums dropped from $720 to $686.

During the last decade, other states have enacted laws to correct what some groups have felt is illegal discrimination built into insurance underwriting practices. A 1985 Montana law, for example, prohibits insurers from charging different rates for insurance, of whatever type, based on the sex or marital status of a policyholder. Hawaii, Massachusetts, Michigan, and North Carolina have similar laws that apply only to auto insurance. Ironically, the very people who hoped to gain from such rules—namely women's groups—have found that their members are paying more for auto insurance. This is because in the past the rates have favored females. As a result, the National Organization for Women

---

PROPOSITION 103

The most publicized auto insurance amendment wasn't passed by a legislature. Proposition 103, a 1988 voter initiative in California, was approved by outraged residents who wanted immediate relief from high insurance costs. To address the concern that drivers are penalized because of where they live, Proposition 103 sought to do away with territorial rating, which was always one of the traditional bases of auto insurance pricing. The initiative also promised to roll back rates for all drivers by 20 percent and to cap insurance company profits.

Proposition 103 also required insurance companies to accept any driver with a clean driving record of three years or more. The initiative provided for an elected, rather than appointed, insurance commissioner to better ensure that consumers' interests come before those of insurance companies.

Unfortunately, over the years the initiative has fallen short of some of its goals. True, premiums have risen less quickly than in the past. California once had the third-highest rate increases in the country; it is now the third lowest. According to California's department of insurance, average annual premiums rose only 2.8 percent in 1992. But today, only 780,000 out of some 20 million California policyholders have received the 20 percent refunds promised by the initiative. The California Supreme Court ruled that insurers don't have to pay the refund if it hurts their bottom line too severely.

(NOW) favors pricing of auto insurance premiums based on the miles a motorist has driven during the past year and not on gender.

Still other state initiatives—notably in California—have focused on creating "no-frills" auto insurance policies for lower-income people. And, of course, there's California's well-known Proposition 103 (see box above).

State Aid to Consumers

States are focusing on other ways to help consumers. Eleven states now have or are developing fraud bureaus, all financed by the insurance industry.

Many states have started consumer hot lines so drivers can complain about their problems with insurance companies. California is planning a toll-free "800" number so consumers can find out which insurers have the best complaint records. Thirty-seven states and the District of Columbia publish auto insurance shopping guides, many with comparisons of premiums for different types of drivers in different counties (see box on page 40).

On the federal level, consumer groups are fighting for the abolition of the insurance industry's exemption from federal antitrust laws. This exemption has enabled competing insurers to share information and use the same sources to formulate the rates on which insurance prices are based. Such a practice is illegal in nearly all other industries.

Currently, financial institutions such as banks also are forbidden by federal law from selling auto insurance. Recent legislative moves to include them in the marketplace might increase competition and lower rates. By one estimate, consumers would save an annual 10 to 15 percent off their insurance premiums if insurers were denied special treatment and forced to compete among themselves and with other sellers of insurance. Federal law, however, does allow states to individually remove the exemption, and some states, including California, are pushing in that direction.

The Insurance Industry Fights Back

The reaction of insurers to government attempts to lower rates has been intense. In California, insurers spent an estimated $100 million to combat Proposition 103. Today, they're still spending millions of dollars battling the initiative's various measures in the courts.

As mentioned before, insurers have reacted to what they feel is unfair regulation by tightening their underwriting standards. Many companies now say they will only give their best rates to drivers with perfect driving records; even a not-at-fault accident can keep a driver off some companies' rolls.

Increasingly, auto insurers—including some of the largest—are trying to abandon the states they find unprofitable. Alternatively, they're not taking on new customers, or they're leaving the auto insurance business entirely.

Despite these changes, state insurance officials say there's no reason for alarm. Many insurers still remain in each state.

Positive Industry Moves. Consumer dissatisfaction with auto insurers has resulted in a few positive responses from the industry. New services have sprung up, such as telephone shopping services for auto insurance. In 1990, too, several insurance industry groups established the National Insurance Consumer Helpline, a toll-free number that consumers can use to answer questions about all lines of property and casualty insurance. The Helpline operates from 8 A.M. to 8 P.M. eastern time, Monday through Friday, at 800-942-4242.

Many insurers, increasingly aware of the costs of maintaining commission agents, are now bypassing that system. Some are establishing or buying "direct-writing" insurance companies that deal with consumers by mail or telephone. Theoretically, the saving from eliminating commissions—as much as 15 percent of the total premium—will be passed on to consumers.

AUTO INSURANCE REFORMS: SOME ANSWERS

Consumers and insurance companies alike are searching for new ways to save money on auto insurance. Many proposals to do this are impractical or too complicated. No-fault insurance, a success in some states, still seems the best solution.

No-Fault: The Real Answer

Nothing would do more to lower auto insurance costs than a complete overhaul of the entire system. Until insurers and legislators take genuine steps to reduce unnecessary claims and lawsuits and wasteful overhead, insuring a car will continue to be a costly burden to most consumers.

The most obvious solution, no-fault insurance, has already been the choice of 13 states: Colorado, Florida, Hawaii, Kansas, Kentucky, Massachusetts, Michigan, Minnesota, New Jersey, New York, North Dakota, Pennsylvania, and Utah. It is also mandated in Puerto Rico. No-fault auto insurance was first introduced in Massachusetts in 1971 as a way to control insurance costs and to make insurance settlements fairer for people who suffer serious injuries. It's still the best answer to keeping auto insurance costs in line.

In a state with a traditional tort liability system, auto accident victims often must sue another person to gain compensation for their own medical expenses and for pain and suffering. The cost of that process—as much as half of which can go toward attorney fees rather than to the victim—contributes to high premiums.

In the states with some form of no-fault insurance, victims are compensated for medical bills by their own insurers, regardless of who was at fault in an accident. In a state with a strong no-fault law, the victim may sue for pain and suffering only in limited circumstances, and not over relatively trivial injuries.

Not all no-fault laws are strict, however. In some cases, successful lobbying by trial lawyers (who have the most to gain from a litigious insurance system) has watered down legislation to the point that costs still remain out of control. In Massachusetts, for example, auto insurance costs are among the highest in the nation. In part, that's because the no-fault law there is weak, allowing victims to sue after accruing just $2,000 in medical bills.

But where strict no-fault laws are in effect, the benefits to consumers are real. In the state of New York, victims can sue only if an accident results in a fracture, dismemberment, significant disfigurement, loss of a body organ, or death. Total premiums in New York are 30 percent lower than they would be without that strict no-fault law, estimates Jeffrey O'Connell, the University of Virginia law professor who pioneered the no-fault concept.

In California and other states, lobbyists for trial attorneys have argued that no-fault is unfair to accident victims because it limits their right to sue. But a study in 1992 by Rand, a California think tank, said the tort system is itself unfair, paying too much to victims with minor injuries and not enough to those suffering major ones. The study said no-fault would reduce the inequities and save California consumers about 12 percent on their premiums.

In three states (Kentucky, New Jersey,

and Pennsylvania), motorists have an interesting choice. They can keep their option to sue for pain and suffering, or they can agree to sue only in extreme cases involving serious injury or death. Consumers who choose the latter no-fault option can save an average of $225 per vehicle annually in New Jersey and $150 in Pennsylvania. In Kentucky, however, the savings are minimal.

O'Connell, who champions the choice system, argues that motorists who want to save money will opt for no-fault, thus reducing the number of lawsuits and the overall cost of awards for pain and suffering. As those costs go down, insurers will pass on their savings in lower premiums for both no-fault coverage and for full-tort coverage. The validity of O'Connell's theory, however, has yet to be proven over time.

Group Auto Insurance

Another solution is to sell auto insurance to groups of people, not to individuals, just as health insurance can be sold to groups through employers or other organizations. Or, alternatively, a large group of people with the same characteristics could be insured by one company. Insurers would save money through lower processing costs and overhead, which then could be passed on in lower premiums to consumers.

To some degree, this idea is already being implemented. Several of the insurers listed in the *Consumer Reports* Ratings (see Appendix A) sell only to people in certain areas, occupations, or ages. The concept could be significantly ex-

panded, however, leading to lower costs for most drivers.

Pay-at-the-Pump Concept

Another intriguing proposal incorporates both no-fault insurance and group insurance. Advocated and popularized by financial writer Andrew Tobias, the *pay-at-the-pump* system has attracted widespread attention.

For about 40 cents more per gallon, Tobias proposes, motorists could get auto insurance that covered liability completely and included coverage for medical benefits and long-term disability—when they bought their gasoline. The coverage could include basic, no-frills collision insurance, and also pay a modest pain-and-suffering benefit for people seriously injured in an accident. Drivers would buy coverage every time they filled up their tanks.

The pay-at-the-pump proposal is based on the proven underwriting theory that the more people drive, the more likely they are to have an accident. Therefore, people who drive more and consume more gasoline will also be paying for more insurance to cover their potential accidents. Inequities could be corrected by surcharges on traffic tickets, car registrations, and drivers' license fees. Bad drivers could pay even more to cover the extra costs of their claims, through hefty surcharges on their traffic tickets, for example.

When you bought insurance at the pump, you'd be purchasing unlimited no-fault protection and unlimited disability and medical coverage. You would also purchase basic collision coverage, probably with a high deductible—perhaps $500—or at a percentage of the car's current market value. If you wanted additional coverage, or comprehensive coverage, you could buy it from a private company. Like flight insurance, this additional coverage might not be a great buy, but it would be available for those who wanted it.

Although the premiums would be collected by the government, the actual coverage would be provided by private insurers. Insurance companies that bid with the state to offer the lowest-cost, most efficient service could provide the insurance. Motorists would be placed in heterogeneous groups of, say, 5,000, and private insurers could bid on the group they wished to service. If the service of the carrier were poor, drivers could complain to the state, which then could punish the insurer by dropping it as a carrier.

In 1993, California legislators seri-

HOW HEALTH INSURANCE CHANGES COULD REDUCE AUTO INSURANCE COSTS

As of this writing, the Clinton administration is formulating proposals to remake the nation's health insurance system. Included in the proposals are changes in auto insurance coverage that, if implemented, could significantly reduce the cost of auto insurance.

Specifically, the plan proposes to include the medical portions of auto insurance—bodily injury liability, personal-injury protection (PIP), and medical payments insurance—among the basic coverages provided under comprehensive health insurance. In other words, injured motorists would not be reimbursed for medical costs by both their health insurer and auto insurer, as is allowed in some states now. Instead, the health insurer would provide all medical coverage for auto-related injuries.

Both insurers and consumer activists agree that the elimination of *double-dipping*—getting reimbursements from two sources—could ultimately reduce auto insurance premiums substantially, although how much would depend on the way premiums are collected for the medical portion of the coverage. Naturally, insurers would like to continue collecting the medical premiums (and the commissions). A State Farm official estimates that changes resulting from the elimination of double-dipping could result in a net savings of $7 billion a year, but it is not clear how much each consumer would save.

According to the National Insurance Consumer Organization, consumers could save more if the premiums were collected in some form of payroll deduction, bypassing the insurers and all their attendant costs. Under such a plan, it estimates that the average consumer could save from 20 percent to 33 percent off the total auto insurance premium.

ously considered a bill to introduce a similar plan, but it failed to pass the legislature. Proponents of the bill claimed that it could save consumers nationwide some $13 billion a year, or 18 percent of the current system. In California alone, they said, motorists could save an estimated $4 billion.

There are many advantages to pay-at-the-pump. First, most of the savings would come from the elimination of selling costs, but some would arise from the greater efficiency that a large system can offer. Second, all motorists would be covered to some degree. The nearly 25 percent of California motorists who drive without insurance would have at least the minimum liability coverage to protect themselves and anyone they hit. Third, a no-fault system built into the pay-at-the-pump concept would reduce the number of frivolous lawsuits that help make insurance so expensive. Finally, the resulting higher cost of a gallon of gasoline might encourage motorists to drive less, which could reduce traffic congestion and improve air quality.

All auto insurance pricing is based on the principle that you pay more when you're exposed to more risks. In the second part of this book, we show you how to minimize that exposure, lower your accident potential, and in the process decrease your auto insurance costs.

PART TWO

HOW TO DRIVE DEFENSIVELY

—

8

Rules of the Road: Safety First

—

Everytime you take the wheel and join the traffic flow, you are entering a complex environment, one with its own rules, regulations, and requirements. It can be a dangerous world, too, when the controls that govern traffic and the smooth operating of the nation's highways are violated or ignored.

VIOLATIONS AND ACCIDENTS

A license to drive a private passenger car is a privilege granted to you by the state in which you reside—a privilege that can be suspended or revoked. A *suspension* is for a specific period of time. A *revocation* is a complete cancellation. In the case of revocation, the state department of motor vehicles will determine whether and when you are eligible to apply for a new license.

Suspensions and revocations may be required by law in the following cases:

- Operating or permitting operation of an uninsured vehicle. The license revocation is for a minimum of one year in many states.
- Multiple speeding or other moving violations occurring within a certain period (18 months in New York State). The license suspension is often for a six-month period.
- Alcohol and drug violations. The length of time for the suspension and revocation may depend on the degree of the driver's impairment. Penalties may also include fines and jail sentences.

Drunk-Driving Violations

Driving while under the influence of alcohol or drugs is an especially serious violation. Chemical test laws as written

THE EFFECTS OF ALCOHOL

Blood-alcohol content (BAC) as a percentage is the measure used to determine both driving while ability-impaired (DWAI) and driving while intoxicated (DWI) levels. Generally, drivers are considered DWI if their BAC is .10 percent or more; a DWAI driver has a BAC of .05 to .09 percent.

The greater the blood-alcohol content, the greater the impairment: Reflexes and reaction time are slowed, the ability to see clearly is reduced, judgment of speed and distance is distorted, and alertness is compromised.

Blood-alcohol content percentage varies not only with the amount of alcohol consumed but also by weight. The slighter your build, the faster you will become intoxicated. As few as two drinks may impair your ability to drive. Note, too, that a drink may be one bottle of beer, one glass of wine, or a single ounce of whiskey—it's the amount of alcohol in the beverage that counts, not the amount of beverage consumed. The number of hours between drinks is also a factor. Only the passage of time lowers blood-alcohol content—there is no shortcut to sobering up.

The following chart shows the correlation of body weight and alcohol content of various drinks in contributing to impairment and intoxication.

ALCOHOL AND BODY WEIGHT

Body Weight	Drinks (Two-Hour Period)											
100	1	2	3	4	5	6	7	8	9	10	11	12
120	1	2	3	4	5	6	7	8	9	10	11	12
140	1	2	3	4	5	6	7	8	9	10	11	12
160	1	2	3	4	5	6	7	8	9	10	11	12
180	1	2	3	4	5	6	7	8	9	10	11	12
200	1	2	3	4	5	6	7	8	9	10	11	12
220	1	2	3	4	5	6	7	8	9	10	11	12
240	1	2	3	4	5	6	7	8	9	10	11	12

BAC = Blood Alcohol Content	Caution: Keep your BAC below .04%	DWAI: Above .05%	DWI: .10% and up

There are solutions to the drinking and driving problem. The "designated driver" strategy, for example, can work well for a group of friends: One member of the group who refrains from drinking alcohol is responsible for the driving. This popular technique is used in many countries to avoid accidents. Alternatively, if you drink, consider staying overnight at your host's home or using public transportation.

by the states vary somewhat, but all have an *implied consent* provision, which means that failure to submit to chemical tests for suspected intoxication will result in automatic license suspension or revocation.

Length of time for suspension or revocation of license, fines, and jail time levied for drivers found guilty of alcohol and drug-related violations may depend on the degree of intoxication, and those periods increase for repeat offenders.

Typical penalties are indicated by the following examples for New York State: Driving while ability-impaired (DWAI) can result in a fine up to $350, jail time up to 15 days, and license suspension for 90 days for a first offense. For a third offense within 10 years, the fine can increase to $1,500, jail to 90 days, and license revocation for at least six months.

The penalties for driving while intoxicated (DWI) are more severe, starting with jail time up to one year and a minimum six-month license revocation. In cases of fatal accidents, a driver may be convicted of vehicular manslaughter or assault, with a jail term of up to seven years.

Moving Violations

Motor vehicle departments keep track of drivers who accumulate traffic violations within a short period of time by using a point system. Points are assigned depending on the seriousness of the violation, and the amount of points is monitored. If the points charged exceed a certain number (usually within a period

of 18 months), drivers face suspension or revocation of their license. The following chart shows typical points assigned for violations in New York State:

POINT SYSTEM FOR MOVING VIOLATIONS

Violation	Points
Speeding (mph over posted limit)	
1 to 10	3
11 to 20	4
21 to 30	6
31 to 40	8
over 40	11
Reckless driving	5
Failing to stop for school bus	5
Following too closely (tailgating)	4
Inadequate brakes in operator's vehicle	4
While driving employer's vehicle	2
Failing to yield right-of-way	3
Violation involving traffic signal, stop sign, or yield sign	3
Railroad crossing violation	3
Improper passing or lane use	3
Leaving scene of an incident involving property damage or injury to animal	3
Child safety restraint violation	3
Any other moving violation	2

Source: New York State Department of Motor Vehicles

TRAFFIC RULES AND REGULATIONS

Each state establishes its own regulations regarding the operation of motor vehicles on its highways. In the absence of nationwide regulations or a uniform traffic code, it is your responsibility to know the traffic rules—not only for your own state but for other states in which you may be driving.

Although many states have established identical rules governing traffic flow, the differences in some states (especially those bordering each other) can be vexing—particularly if you first learn of the rule when you get a ticket for violating it.

The rule for passing on the right, for example, differs slightly between New York State and Connecticut. In New York, passing on the right is allowed on roads with *two* lanes of traffic moving in that direction. Connecticut, however, specifies that you must be on a road where *three* or more lanes of traffic are moving in the same direction.

Other regulations set by the states govern virtually every aspect of driving; there are rules for roadways and vehicles as well as rules specifying the responsibilities of drivers. A sampling of those regulations, many of which differ from state to state, follow:

- *Speed limits.* Besides the national speed limit of 55 mph and some 65-mph limits on interstates, there are speed limits for local roads, school zones, and so on. Where a limit is not posted, motorists are required to drive at a "reasonable" rate of speed.
- *Radar detectors.* Detectors are legal in all states, except for Virginia and the District of Columbia.
- *Seat belts and child restraints.* Most states and the District of Columbia have safety belt laws. Exceptions are Kentucky, Maine, Massachusetts, New Hampshire, North Dakota, South Dakota, Vermont, and West Virginia. (Some of these states are introducing or have enacted legislation for the mandatory use of seat belts.)

In most states, these laws cover front-seat occupants only. In addition, drivers are responsible for proper restraints for children, usually those between 4 and 16 years old sitting in the front seats. And all 50 states and the District of Columbia now have laws requiring infants and small children to be restrained in infant carriers or special safety seats. Again, the driver is responsible for adhering to the law.

Fines levied for violations of seat belt and child restraint laws are low—$10 to $25 for seat belts and $25 to $50 for child restraints. In most states, motorists must have committed some other moving violation before they can be ticketed for failure to buckle up.

- *Headlight use.* Drivers are required to turn on headlights, usually from one-half hour after sunset to one-half hour before sunrise—and whenever light conditions restrict visibility. New York State, for one, requires lights on when wipers are on. Unfortunately, not all states *require* headlights to be on in rain, sleet, and snow, but most states permit driving with headlights on during the day. Bumper stickers seen on many interstate trucks tell you why: "Lights on for Safety."

- *Bare feet and left feet.* Most states allow driving with bare feet and permit left-foot braking of cars with automatic transmissions.

- *Hand signals.* Automatic turn signals have made hand signals almost obsolete. Nevertheless, hand signals have their place. A right turn is signaled by arm upward, left turn by horizontal, and slow or stop by arm downward. Automatic turn signals are required when a vehicle is so loaded or constructed as to obscure the driver's hand signals.

- *School buses.* You are required to stop when school buses are loading and unloading. You are not to proceed until the bus resumes motion or the driver signals to proceed. If the stopped bus is on the opposite side of a dual highway divided by a median strip, you need not stop. In most cases, flashing lights on the bus will signal that it is stopped.

- *No-passing zones.* These are indicated by a solid line and a solid line on the driver's side of the dotted line. These zones are usually indicated by roadside signs as well.

- *Stops at railroad crossings.* You are required to stop at railway crossings when alerted by warning signals. School buses, commercial vehicles transporting explosives or flammable liquids, and liveries carrying passengers for hire are required to come to a full stop before crossing the tracks.

- *Auxiliary driving lights.* Check your state's regulations, which may be quite detailed, on permitted car lights. Nevada, for example, allows a vehicle to have two driving lamps, two passing lamps, two fog lamps, and two spot lamps, as long as not more than four lamps (including head lamps) are lighted at one time, if each projects a beam intensity greater than 300 candlepower.

- *Seals and stickers.* Windshield stickers are usually prohibited unless they are official. Some state regulations are very specific for unofficial stickers: In Virginia, a sticker may not exceed 2½ inches in width and 4 inches in length and must be positioned in the blind spot behind the rearview mirror. Common sense dictates that stickers, dangling baby shoes, or toys attached with suction cups should not obstruct the driver's vision on side or rear windows.

- *Tinted glass.* A recent phenomenon is the application of glass-tinting products on the inside of car windows that all but conceal the occupants of a car. Some states prohibit tinting that's too dark. In Oregon, any such use is illegal. In some states, the tinting material can be applied only to rear side windows, provided the car has two outside rearview mirrors. Tinting on front side windows is illegal in all states.

- *Studded tires.* These inserts, used for snow tires, damage pavement, so their use is usually limited to the winter months. Regular studs are not allowed in some states, only "soft" studs that consist of tungsten carbide fragments in a soft metal matrix. Some states prohibit studs entirely.

- *Towing autos.* In all states, the regulations about towing other vehicles behind a car are quite specific. On some roads, it is not allowed at all. State rules vary concerning the tow connections (rigid, nonrigid, length of connector, safety chains, etc.).

- *Right turn on red.* This rule allows a right turn after a full stop at a traffic light. It speeds traffic flow and saves gas, but safety is compromised when the rule is abused by drivers who don't stop or even slow down before making the right. Right on red is not allowed in some urban areas, such as New York City.

- *Bumper heights.* Some customized cars have higher- or lower-than-usual bumpers. Check with your state department of motor vehicles before altering the bumper height of your car or van. A state's rules can be complex. Utah, for example, sets permissible lift heights by formula, according to wheelbase.

- *Wearing of audio headsets while driving.* It's usually permitted, but keep the volume down, for safety reasons.

- *Alcohol containers.* In most states, transporting an open alcoholic beverage container in a car is illegal.

- *Hazard warning lights.* There are many states—Alaska, Connecticut, Maine, New York, and Pennsylvania, among others—that permit their use by vehicles moving on the highway. Drivers can alert traffic behind to emergencies and supplement their brake lights by turning on hazard flashers. In some states, posted signs mandate their use only by vehicles moving at less than a certain speed.

- *Riding in back of a pickup truck.* This practice is usually forbidden in the more populous states, but riding in the back of an open (unenclosed) pickup is tolerated in western states if passengers sit on the floor.

- *Emergency radio use.* Some states post monitoring of citizens band channel 9 for emergencies.

REDEEMING YOUR RECORD

If you already have a record of convictions and accidents, and you're concerned about the money you pay for insurance (as well as the safety consequences of your driving), you can regain your safe-driving reputation over a period of time.

Usually, a three-year period with no convictions and no accidents will reinstate a clean driving record. In some cases, insurance companies will consider your driving history for a longer period (as long as five years). That may be the case if your record includes license suspensions or revocations for speeding, alcohol and/or drug offenses, or assault.

To keep auto insurance premiums down, you have to learn to drive defensively.

9

Defensive Driving:
Before You Start Out

—

It's an old saw—as old as the 100 years that motor cars have been on the road—but still true: Auto accidents are caused by "the nut behind the wheel." Blaming a mechanical failure for highway accidents is convenient, but in the overwhelming number of crashes, the cause is driver error.

We've all seen accident reports in the press that read: "The car went out of control and crossed the median...." The truth may be that the *driver* lost control. Most likely, the driver failed to handle the car properly in an emergency, perhaps because of inadequate skills or a lapse in concentration. Possibly he or she was under the influence of alcohol or drugs, or was simply reckless.

LEARNING GOOD DRIVING SKILLS

Whether or not you get safely to your destination depends on your skills as a driver, your emotional maturity, the condition of your car, the design of the highways you drive on and, of course, the weather. First and foremost *you* are the most important element in the safety equation. Your attitude, judgment, and skill as a driver outweigh all other considerations.

Attitude

For some drivers, nothing short of a personality change would curb their contribution to the nation's accident rate. The aggressive driver, the hostile driver, the careless driver, and the nervous and timid driver—all are threats to everyone on the road.

A skilled driver can also be a risk-taker, shaving every traffic situation as closely as possible and terrorizing other motorists. Recognizing and avoiding these types of drivers, even if it means surrendering your right-of-way, is an essential part of driving defensively. And here's where attitude comes in again: It's necessary to curb your own aggressive instincts against other drivers on the road. These sometimes hard-to-resist urges are sure paths to an unpleasant altercation or an accident.

Judgment

Most of us know how to anticipate and recognize common accident situations: the ball bouncing into the street (chances are a child will follow). But there are less obvious potential incidents. Professional car racers, for example, may seem reckless, but they are also accomplished in the art of not taking unnecessary risks. Remember, they are rewarded for being precise and fast—not for crashing.

A race driver usually doesn't win by slowing down, but in an extraordinary display of judgment one famous driver—Juan Manuel Fangio—did just that as he approached a high-speed bend in the Grand Prix race at Monte Carlo in 1950. His tip-off to trouble ahead was a visual clue in his peripheral vision: On one lap of the race he missed the play of light on the spectators' faces as he entered this blind curve. Normally, the crowd would be watching him as he approached, admiring his speed and control. His experience and intuition told him that the reason the grandstands appeared darker than usual was because faces were turned *away* from him. Only a major incident around the bend could claim such attention on the part of the crowd. With no other information to go on, he let up on the throttle and began braking. His intuition was correct, and he avoided the pileup that had just

occurred ahead of him on the racetrack.

Good judgment is a race driver's stock-in-trade and can make the difference between winning a race and ending up in a tangled crash. Our highways aren't meant to be racetracks, but all of us can attempt to develop some of the racing car driver's superior concentration and sense of timing.

Skill

Before you can develop the fine art of defensive driving, you must have the confidence to handle an automobile in most situations. This means the ability to maneuver any type of car in all types of traffic, weather, and emergencies.

Good driving requires concentration and quick reflexes. Recent developments in suspension and brake design may only increase the challenge for the person at the controls. The danger lies in being lulled into a false sense of security and invulnerability; unfortunately, modern automobiles make it all too easy to become a passive driver. A skilled driver, on the other hand, knows how to "read the road" and spot accidents in the making.

THE FIRST LINE OF DEFENSE: YOUR AUTO EQUIPMENT

Some safety features are inherent in a car's design, or available as optional equipment. Such items, which can help you avoid an accident, include:

- Suspensions and tires engineered to hold the road
- Quick, precise steering for evasive action
- Low-fade disc brakes and antilock braking system (ABS)
- Good visibility

More subtle contributors to safety help keep a driver alert and comfortable: effective climate control, a wide range of seat adjustments, and convenient placement of instruments and controls.

Some safety features come into play only if your car is in an accident, helping you avoid injury or death. Such features, which contribute to a car's "crashworthiness," include:

- Shatterproof laminated windshield and window glass
- Antiburst door locks that prevent doors from opening in a crash

- Impact-absorbing steering column
- Padded dash and soft instrument-panel controls
- Crumple zones, or an energy-absorbent body structure ahead of and behind the passenger compartment
- Side-impact door beams, to minimize side intrusion in broadside accidents
- Protected fuel tank placement
- Head restraints to protect against whiplash
- Crush-resistant roof designs
- Air bags
- Three-point lap-and-shoulder belts

Federal legislation already requires most of the safety features that improve crashworthiness. (Air bags and manual lap-and-shoulder belts will be mandatory by the 1998 model year.) But not all cars are equally competent in avoiding a crash or protecting their occupants if a

---

REACTION-TIME TEST

A simple test can be quite revealing about your ability to perceive a dangerous situation on the road and react quickly enough to avoid it—either by braking or steering around the problem.

Use this test to check how quickly you react when fresh and rested, when tired, or when you have consumed alcoholic beverages.

Cut and mark an 11-inch strip of heavyweight paper or lightweight cardboard (see illustration). This will serve as a timer. Hold your thumb and forefinger horizontally, with a half-inch space between them. Ask a friend to hold the timer so its lower edge is just above the space between your forefinger and thumb.

Your friend should release the timer without warning. It's up to you to catch the timer with your finger and thumb as quickly as possible. The point at which you do shows your reaction time. A slower reaction means less ability to drive safely.

Source: New York State Department of Motor Vehicles

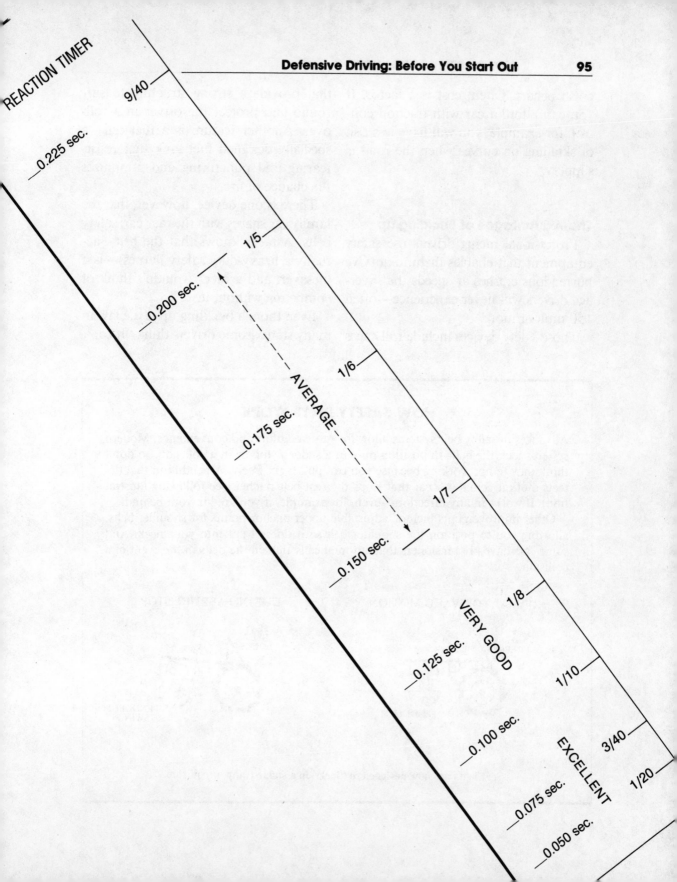

REACTION TIMER

9/40 —
— 0.225 sec.

1/5 —
— 0.200 sec.

1/6 —

AVERAGE

— 0.175 sec.

1/7 —

— 0.150 sec.

1/8 —

VERY GOOD

— 0.125 sec.

1/10 —

— 0.100 sec.

EXCELLENT

3/40 —

— 0.075 sec.

1/20 —

— 0.050 sec.

crash occurs. Often, cost is a factor. If you can afford a car with traction control, for example, you will have less risk of skidding on curves when the road is slippery.

The Advantages of Buckling Up

Professional racing drivers use safety equipment that enables them to survive horrendous crashes at speeds that average drivers will never experience—often 150 mph or more.

Those safety devices include roll cages that provide a strong structure to surround and protect the driver in a rollover. Another feature is a fuel cell—a specially designed fuel tank that resists tearing and puncturing and minimizes the chance of fire.

There is one device, however, that the family car shares with the race car: safety belts. A racer knows that the belt—actually a heavy-duty safety harness—is a lifesaver, and a racer wouldn't think of competing without it.

Even though buckling up is the law in many states, some drivers think "It can't

HOW SAFETY BELTS WORK

Advances in safety belt systems allow for more comfort and convenience. Modern systems lock the belts in position only in a sudden stop or in a collision, so don't think they're not working because you can pull them freely. A pendulum that detects motion actuates a bar that stops the seat belt ratchet (see following illustration). It works in any direction—even, for example, if you are hit from behind.

Other improvements include adjustable upper anchor points for shoulder belts, allowing you to position the shoulder belt so it doesn't cut into your neck. And some cars have pre-tensioners that automatically tighten the belts in the event of a collision.

NORMAL FORWARD MOTION

DURING ABRUPT STOP

Seat belts are now designed to "lock" in a sudden stop or collision.

happen to me." In some cases, however, even the most skilled driver can't avoid an impact. Your best chance of survival is to wear your seat belt.

Unfortunately, some passive belt systems—the type that combines a motorized shoulder belt with a manual lap belt—offer a false sense of security to drivers and front-seat passengers. The automatic movement of the shoulder belt into position across the chest means the manual lap belt may be forgotten or ignored, and the car's front-seat occupants are only half-protected.

Air Bags

One of the major advantages of air bags is that they meet the legal requirement for passive safety without the manufacturer having to resort to half-baked solutions. A car with an air bag allows an automaker to provide manual, three-point shoulder-and-lap belts that are comfortable and easy to use. A quick, one-handed, single motion from shoulder to hip, and—*click*—you're covered with the best protection you can have on the road.

Air bags themselves don't provide protection in all types of accidents. If you are thrown out of your car, suffer a secondary collision with the inside of your car after the initial impact, or experience a neck-snapping tumbling in rollover accidents, only seat belts can protect you. Remember, an air bag is only a supplementary restraint system (this is what "SRS" embossed on the steering-wheel hub means).

KEEPING YOUR CAR SERVICED

To keep the safety odds on your side, make sure that your driving skills are not undermined by a car that has been neglected. Don't trust an annual safety inspection—you should maintain your car and get it serviced more than once a year. That includes oil changes, occasional tune-ups (depending on miles driven), and routine checks on everything from lights to fluids.

Lights

When you slow down and signal traffic behind that you're making a turn, you assume that your rear signal flashers and brake lights are working. But are they? Or is a bulb burned out? Here's a tip for making it easy to periodically check your lights—and you don't even have to get out of your car. Put on the brakes and flashers in a dimly lit garage. The glow of the lights will be obvious, if they're working properly. Or, in a shopping area, face a store window. Test your front lights, flashers, headlights, high beams, and fog lights. The window will reflect the lights.

Tires

Check that your car's tire pressures are to specification—that is, inflated to the pounds per square inch recommended in your owner's manual. Low tire pressure adversely affects the handling of the car, wears tires prematurely, and reduces fuel mileage because of increased friction between the tires and the road. Check for pressure before and after a long trip, and in between while filling up the gas tank.

Fluids

In winter, your visibility can drop almost to zero if the wipers are smearing the windshield and the windshield-washer reservoir is empty. Keep the reservoir full, and check other fluids when you're under the hood: engine oil, transmission fluid, brake fluid, coolant, and battery electrolyte. Or ask your mechanic to check for you.

Keep a Maintenance Record

Proper maintenance is not only vital for the life of your car, but for your safety as well. Keep a small logbook in your glove compartment, and use it to note the date and mileage for all parts replacements, regular maintenance, and repairs. Keep track of the mileage intervals at which your front brake pads need replacing, when you last rotated tires, how often you're adding engine oil—ev-

erything about your car's health. While you're at it, keep a check on fuel mileage and car costs. Such a record will increase the value of your car when you sell it.

BEFORE YOU DRIVE: KNOW YOUR CAR

Familiarity with a car is essential for safe driving, especially its acceleration, handling, and braking ability. Know the car you're driving, and adjust your driving technique accordingly. The amount of acceleration on tap can get you out of certain emergencies—often at intersections and in merging with traffic. Also important are braking distances, which is consumer information that the manufacturer must disclose with all new vehicles. In practice, though, drivers get to know their cars in everyday driving.

Features can affect handling. For example, does the car have front-wheel drive or rear-wheel drive? On slippery roads and during hard cornering, the two designs can handle quite differently.

WHAT COLOR IS YOUR CAR?

The color of a car is not normally associated with safety. Studies show, however, that the color white is actually a safety feature because it gives you visibility to other drivers on the road. In other words, you are *noticed*.

The best color for visibility is classic white, then the yellows, ivories, and beiges. The worst colors for visibility are black, and the sky and earth colors: deep blues, greens, and browns.

So, if you want to stand out from the crowd when you buy your next car, choose safety over fashion.

In extremely windy weather, a van may be difficult to keep within your lane because of the larger profile the vehicle presents to the gusts. The steering response of a large car or van also may be slower than that of a smaller car.

GETTING COMFORTABLE AT THE WHEEL

You can't practice good driving techniques if you're not properly seated at the steering wheel, with all the controls and adjustments set for your height and reach. Use the seat adjustments—and the telescoping and height positions for the steering wheel, if your car has them—to position yourself within comfortable reach of all floor pedals. You should be at a distance from the steering wheel that allows your arms to bend slightly at the elbows. Grip the wheel with both hands, with thumbs around the wheel at roughly the 10 and 2 o'clock positions.

HEAD RESTRAINTS

Head restraints must bolster the back of the head (not the neck) if they are to protect against whiplash. Check the position of the restraint before you drive. After checking seat position, mirrors, and all the controls and instruments in front of you, make it a habit to move your head rearward to make sure the restraint is where it's supposed to be.

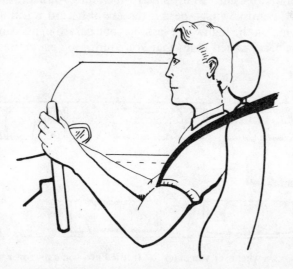

Head restraints should be positioned high enough to support the back of the head.

Then, secure your position at the wheel by fastening your safety belt.

Safety Belts

Position the safety belt with the lap belt low, across the hips, and the shoulder belt across shoulder and chest. The point is to prevent the pressure of an impact from being transmitted to internal organs: The hip and pelvis area and the shoulder, breastbone, and ribs can withstand impact pressure better than the organs in the abdomen.

A pregnant woman should always wear the lap-and-shoulder belt.

LIGHTS ARE LIFESAVERS

A simple collision preventer, especially on residential streets where cars are parked on both sides, is to always signal when leaving the curb. A flashing light will be seen by oncoming drivers and your intentions will be known.

Headlight flashers are also effective in communicating on the road—to flash oncoming drivers when you're out of your lane and going around a road obstacle, to get the attention of drivers who pull out in front of you, or to signal oncoming drivers that their lights should be on.

Hazard lights, or four-way flashers, are another important safety feature. In fact, the switch marked with the red triangle is one of the first you should find among your car's controls. Use it when your car is disabled—especially if you are unable to move out of a traffic lane. Many states—including Alaska, Connecticut, Maine, New York, and Pennsylvania—permit the use of hazard warning lights while the vehicle is moving on the highway. Flashing your hazard lights can alert other drivers to trouble ahead, or tell them that you are having some mechanical or other problem.

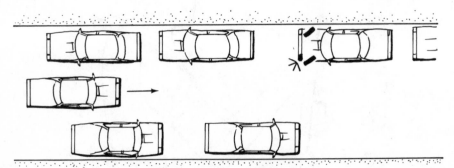

Use your turn signals whenever you enter the traffic flow—on a narrow residential street, for example.

Mirrors

Set mirrors to give you the widest angle of visibility without having to turn your head. Many drivers prefer to adjust the left mirror so they can see just a bit of the side of the car, for better orientation.

Don't hang decorations and souvenirs from the center mirror. And don't hang clothing from the hook over the right rear window. A dangling coat or dress limits your visibility. Hang them instead on the driver's side.

Head Restraints

Most cars have adjustable head restraints, but too often they are not set properly. They should be high enough that the center of the restraint is even with your ears. Only then will it be able to do its job of protecting you against neck injuries if you are hit from the rear.

Other Safety Precautions

Make sure that loose luggage is safely stowed in the trunk of the car, or tied down if it's in a station wagon. Remove all objects from a sedan's rear window shelf. They can become projectiles in an accident.

Always drive with your doors locked. In a rollover accident, locked doors are more likely to stay closed, and to contribute to the ability of the passenger compartment to resist crushing. It's also a precaution against crime.

Lights On

Headlights are not just for seeing where you're going but also to allow other drivers to see you. In some parts of the world—notably Canada and the Scandinavian countries—running lights are now required in latest-model cars. Those lights are wired to the ignition so they're on whenever the car is running.

It makes good sense to turn on the headlights not only at dusk, dawn, and at night, but whenever the weather reduces visibility. "Headlights on when windshield wipers are on" is the wording in some states. To be even safer, turn on your lights whenever the day is gray and overcast, even if the wipers are not in use.

10

Safe Driving Techniques: On the Road

—

Defensive driving is simply a way to avoid other drivers who might run into you. But avoiding disaster on the road involves much more than just a gut reaction to danger.

If an accident does occur, perhaps it's because you put yourself in a vulnerable position—because the other driver didn't see you, or your signals were faulty and misled the driver behind you, or you were tailgating the vehicle in front of you.

Here we'll discuss the fine points of sharing the road with other drivers as well as how various car handling techniques can save you from traffic citations and accidents. These tips can also help you avoid increases in your auto insurance premiums.

EVERYDAY DRIVING STRATEGIES

We often take driving for granted: Turn the key, step on the accelerator, and off we go. Our driving motions become second nature, and we do them almost automatically—until something goes wrong. It could happen when you are merging with traffic, changing lanes, or turning left at an intersection. Then you need to consider your options, fast.

Merging and Highway Driving

Ever try jumping onto a moving carousel or merry-go-round? You can't get aboard from a dead stop; you've got to get up to speed before making your move. It's much the same situation when a driver has to merge with moving traffic, especially on ramps of limited-access parkways and freeways.

According to the Federal Highway Administration, fewer accidents occur on these limited-access roads than on other highways. Yet many inexperienced drivers are intimidated when merging with flowing traffic. (In some parts of the country, a traffic-light system feeds cars at intervals into the merge lane, to avoid pileups.)

Merging doesn't have to be hard on the nerves, but it does have its perils. At merges, look out for the impatient, tailgating driver in the merge lane who suddenly swings out onto the main highway by crossing solid pavement markings. Also, steer clear of those drivers who merge and then continue crossing traffic to move immediately to the center or left lane. These reckless drivers interfere with the traffic flow and set up potential accidents.

Multilane driving has its own safety rules and disciplines. If you are driving on a three-lane highway, for example, be cautious when moving into the center lane from the right lane. A driver in the left lane may have the same idea. Also, try to avoid getting stuck in a "pack" where cars are tailgating. One mistake and the resulting accident can involve many cars across several lanes.

On multilane highways, keep to the right except when passing. Using the passing lane as a through lane disrupts traffic flow and creates impatient drivers behind you. Slower drivers should *always* keep to the extreme right lane. Always signal a lane change, and always turn your head quickly to check your "blind" spot and use your sideview mirrors.

Avoid sudden lane changes by positioning your car for left- and right-hand turns well ahead of the intersection or exit. If you miss your turn or exit, continue on to the next one; don't jeopardize yourself or others by braking suddenly, stopping, or—most dangerous of all—backing up.

Some limited-access highways are open to all traffic; on others, commercial vehicles are forbidden. Certainly, it is less stressful to drive on parkways that ban commercial vans and trucks, especially those big rigs and semis that are prone to "jackknifing."

On commercial routes, avoid the big rigs as much as possible. Never drive into a truck's blind spots: directly behind the truck and at its left and right sides. When passing a truck, do it quickly: A truck driver who doesn't see you on the left or right may decide to change lanes, not realizing that you're there. Large, heavy trucks and buses take longer to stop, so keep your distance. Stay away from flatbed and other trucks that might scatter poorly secured cargo or dump debris on cars behind them.

Use Your Mirrors

When you drive, use your rearview mirrors. Ideally, there are three, one on each side of the car and, of course, the center mirror. Practice using them, shift-

MERGE AND LANE CHANGE

In merging or switching lanes, avoid disturbing the traffic flow. Drivers with "I'm-the-only-car-on-the-road" syndrome cause other drivers to suddenly slow down, speed up, or change lanes. The resulting turbulence in the traffic flow can cause accidents.

On the entrance ramp of a parkway, signal and merge at the first opportunity. Use the ramp to accelerate to near traffic speed while selecting a gap to fit into. At the same time, monitor the traffic on the ramp ahead and behind you. If traffic is so heavy that you cannot join the flow, then stop in time to leave yourself enough room on the ramp for another try. Be careful of risk-takers who may try to drive around you on the ramp. When you merge, stay in the right lane; signal and move to a passing lane only after you are moving with traffic and observe that the lane is clear of faster traffic. Before moving to the center lane of a three-lane parkway, always signal, use your mirrors, and quickly turn your head to check your blind spots. Watch out for other vehicles that may also be changing lanes.

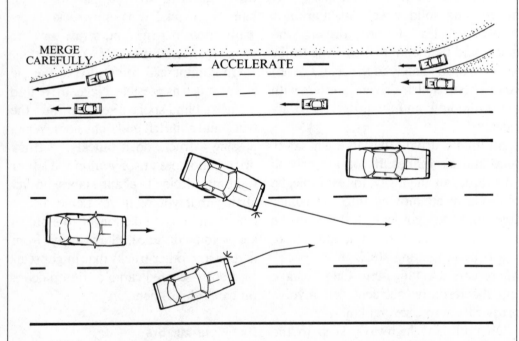

Merges and lane changes must be timed, coordinated, and executed with judgment and an awareness of the traffic around you.

ing your eyes frequently so as not to miss any traffic. To detect traffic at your left and right sides—your so-called blind spots—you must move your head to check, but quickly, without taking your eyes off the road for more than a second or two.

When scanning the road ahead, don't neglect to check for cars approaching you from the side. This can be especially dangerous on those suburban neighborhood cross streets where the stop signs are placed facing a different direction at each intersection (see following box). Always slow down enough to see that the road is clear right and left wherever you are not required to come to a stop. Be prepared to stop in case someone runs the stop sign.

Braking in an Emergency

If you hit another vehicle in the front or side, or collide with a bicyclist, pedestrian, animal, or stationary object, it may or may not be your fault. It's always your fault, however, if you hit another car from behind.

Stopping your car or slowing quickly enough to avoid hitting something or someone requires more than just pressing down hard on the brake pedal and hanging on. Unless your car has an antilock braking system, standing on your brakes can lock up your wheels, preventing you from steering.

That's why skilled drivers rapidly *pump* their brakes during emergency slowing or stopping on slippery roads. You avoid locking the wheels, and you

have a better chance of keeping your car from skidding or spinning out. In many situations, steering *around* an obstacle may be safer than hard braking.

Of course, if your car has an antilock brake system (ABS), you can keep your foot on the brake pedal and the wheels won't lock. (The pulsing you feel at the pedal when the ABS goes into operation is the electronic "pumping" that alternately applies and releases the brakes so steering control is retained.)

Similarly, if in midcorner you find yourself going too fast, ease off the throttle but *don't* brake. Maintain a steady speed and steer smoothly through the turn. Again, if your car has antilock brakes, you can brake and steer at the same time.

Take a tip from aviation safety: Pilots are not allowed to fly a specific aircraft until they've been in a simulator, which subjects them to any emergencies that could occur in the air. Get to know your car in a similar way. On a safe stretch of wet pavement, apply the brakes and feel how the pedal pulses, which indicates that your antilock braking system is working to keep you from skidding. Steer at the same time you are braking hard, so you know how it feels. Do the same with your traction control, so you know the system's capability. In this way, you can develop the confidence you need in an emergency.

If Your Brakes Fail

Complete brake failure is an uncommon occurrence today, especially with

CAUTION ON CROSS STREETS

Residential neighborhoods with a grid of cross streets can require extra alertness when the stop signs alternate facing directions—and if the cross streets are not four-way-stop intersections (see illustration). Always be prepared to stop when approaching an intersection, even if the cross traffic has stop signs. Drivers who don't stop, whether it's because of inattention or recklessness, can broadside or "T-bone" your car. This is one of the most serious types of accidents, in which seat belts and air bags have little effect in reducing injury.

When driving in such areas, it is always helpful to leave your window open to hand-signal other drivers. Indecisive or impatient drivers may stop at the cross street about the same time you do. Wave them on rather than risk a fender bender or worse.

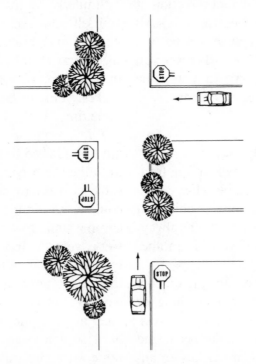

Use caution approaching all intersections in case cross traffic does not observe stop signs or signals.

STEER CLEAR

On the road, always be ready to take evasive action. When you cannot stop in time, you may be able to steer around an obstacle. This maneuver also will alert drivers behind you, and may save you from being rear-ended.

Alternating braking and steering, sometimes called *cadence braking,* allows the car's wheels to roll between stabs at the brakes, so you can steer around the obstacle. Antilock braking systems (ABS) allow you to steer while the brake pedal is continuously depressed.

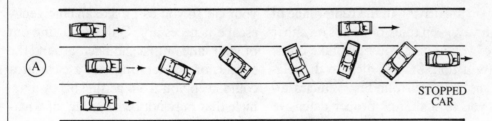

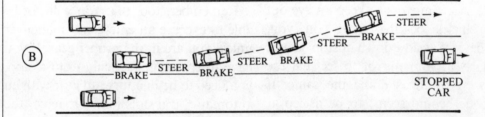

To retain steering control of your car, do not lock up brakes. With locked braking (A), you may skid and be unable to steer clear. With cadence braking (B), you may be able to steer around the obstacle.

modern dual-circuit systems, where one set of hydraulic brake lines activates the brakes if the other fails. But if you do lift your foot from the gas and press the brake pedal and nothing happens, you have to make many quick decisions.

Start by pumping the pedal to try to regain hydraulic pressure. At the same time, downshift to a lower gear. If you feel no braking effect at the pedal, apply the emergency, or parking, brake *with care*—you don't want to induce a skid. The combination of the emergency brake and the transmission's lower gears (whether manual or automatic) may be enough to slow you to a stop.

Meanwhile, you have to continue steering the car. You may be able to steer along the shoulder of the road until you stop, or pull off on an uphill slope. In a dire emergency, try to lessen your speed by riding along a guard rail or sideswiping bushes or other obstacles.

How to Avoid Getting Hit from Behind

If you are driving in the center lane of a highway, keep track of what's on either side of you in case you must take quick evasive action. Staying alert to the relative speeds of surrounding vehicles allows you to make the proper defensive moves.

Too often, even good drivers miss what's happening behind them. Always use rearview mirrors to keep an eye out for vehicles bearing down on you. Whenever you slow down or stop, glance regularly in your mirror to see that the following traffic is doing the same. If someone behind seems to be asleep at the wheel, or too close, slow down more gradually and pump your brakes to alert the driver. (Note that on many long uphill grades where an extra right-hand lane is provided for slow traffic—mostly trucks—posted signs instruct drivers to "Use Flashers Below 40 mph.")

When coming to a full stop at a traffic light or stop sign, or for backed-up traffic, always leave some room ahead of your car so you can make an emergency escape if necessary. Quickly darting out of your lane onto a shoulder, around the corner, or accelerating into a clear area could keep you from getting hit by a vehicle that may not be stopping for whatever reason. Keep an eye on your rearview mirror until you observe that all traffic behind you has stopped.

Remember, too, that you will not be able to execute an emergency maneuver unless you are in the proper gear. If you have to speed up suddenly from a stop, you need to be in a forward gear with an automatic transmission, or have the

---

IF YOUR CAR LOSES POWER

There's no more helpless feeling than having your car lose power while you're driving on a highway. You put your foot down on the accelerator and nothing happens. If that occurs, the only advantage you have is your speed. Put your emergency flashers on, open the driver's window so you can hand-signal other drivers, shift out of forward gear (to disconnect the braking effect of the engine), and take advantage of whatever forward motion you have to coast to safety. Do *not* turn off your ignition, which would lock your steering wheel and make operating your power steering and brakes much more difficult.

It's most important to get out of the traffic lanes as soon as you are able to. Worry about restarting the car after you are safely off the road.

clutch depressed and be in first gear with a manual. Similarly, when you are slowing for a turn or parkway exit, brake and downshift before the turn for better control.

The Half-Second Advantage. Most of the millions of rear-end collisions that occur every year could be prevented if people kept their eyes on the road instead of daydreaming, turning their heads to talk, or adjusting the radio or car phone.

Researchers studying the causes of rear-end collisions have found that had the driver behind had an extra half-second to react, most of those accidents could have been prevented.

Radar detection, in its most sophisticated form, may be part of a future warning system that could activate a car's brakes in the event of hazards appearing on the road ahead. Until such a safety option is available, however, there's only one way to avoid a rear-ender: Concentrate on your driving.

Safe at Any Speed

The national speed limit is 55 mph (with some 65-mph exceptions), but driving even at that speed is illegal under certain circumstances. Citations for driving "too fast for conditions" are usually issued to drivers who do not take the weather or traffic into account and persist in maintaining the maximum allowable speed despite reduced visibility and traction. Other factors as well determine a safe cruising speed.

The most skilled driver, for example, cannot fully compensate for a car that is below par in performance. It may be old or in poor mechanical condition, perhaps with worn tires. You cannot keep up with the flow of traffic in a potentially malfunctioning vehicle.

A car that is heavily loaded with passengers and luggage will need longer to stop. Traffic volume must be considered. A driver who is navigating unfamiliar roads will also have to reduce speed. And reducing speed may be necessary when faced with the glare of a setting sun, or while driving at night.

Finally, motorists who have passengers in the car must consider their comfort. It's not fair to subject passengers to what they may perceive as risks.

The Psychological Speed Trap

The time saved by driving faster is often insignificant. For example, driving at 65 mph for 20 miles, instead of at 55 mph, saves you only about three minutes.

To some drivers, of course, speeding has nothing to do with getting somewhere fast. These people enjoy the sense of competing against other drivers and the danger that accompanies cutting corners and defying authority. Again, be a defensive driver and stay out of the way of stoplight drag racers.

Night and Bad Weather Driving

Night driving, even in clear weather, has its own hazards. Not the least is the possible presence on the road of drunk

AVOIDING A HEAD-ON CRASH

The nightmare of all drivers is an oncoming vehicle entering their lane without warning. A skilled driver can take action to minimize the impact or, with both skill and luck, avoid it altogether.

On a two-lane road (see illustration below), scan the road well ahead. Flash headlights if an oncoming driver appears to be drifting toward you, then slow down (to reduce closing speed between the two vehicles). Always steer toward the right shoulder, so if you do hit the vehicle, you will suffer a sideswipe rather than a head-on collision. If necessary, drive off the road. On multilane roadways, drive in the right lane to allow yourself more time to act.

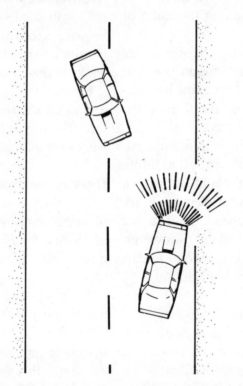

Quick action must be taken to avoid a head-on crash.

drivers. Fatal crashes occur more often during hours of darkness than during the day, and more often on the weekends. If you must drive at night, or in poor weather, observe the following cautions:

Maintain Visibility. Almost all driving decisions are based on what your eyes tell you, so make sure nothing compromises your visibility at night in any way. Keep the windshield clean, and make

ROOM FOR ESCAPE

Always leave enough space between your car and other vehicles ahead. Your only chance of avoiding being hit from the rear is to have enough room to accelerate ahead and get to a shoulder or even around a corner. Don't get pinned in.

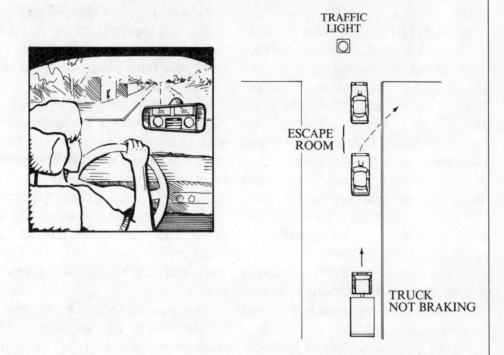

TRAFFIC LIGHT

ESCAPE ROOM

TRUCK NOT BRAKING

Always monitor traffic behind your car; last-minute action could prevent a rear-ender.

sure your windshield wipers are in good working order. Keep your headlights adjusted and your headlight lenses clean so the full light output reaches the road. (The importance of clean lenses now is recognized as a safety factor, so more new cars come equipped with headlight wipers or high-pressure cleaning nozzles.)

Don't wear tinted lenses or sunglasses at night, and avoid staring directly at the lights of oncoming cars. Minimize glare by keeping your car's interior dome light off and using the night position of your rearview mirror. Compensate for reduced visibility at night by driving more slowly and by not "overdriving" your headlights—that is, driving too fast to be able to stop within the distance illuminated by your lights. Use your high beams only when there is no oncoming traffic, to avoid blinding other drivers.

Your own high beams can also blind you. In fog and driving snow, especially, light reflected back from high beams can interfere with your ability to see. The proper lighting for fog is from headlight low beams (so other drivers can see you) and from the high-intensity rear fog light (if your car has one). Make sure your visibility is not reduced by a misty windshield: Turn on wipers, and set climate-control defogging to maximum. If you must slow down rapidly when hitting thick fog or when running into a dust storm, use your four-way flashers while you pull off the road. Parking off the highway, however, is no guarantee of safety, so use extreme caution.

Preventing pileups of cars and trucks in thick fog is difficult, mainly because individual drivers' responses to a sudden blindness is unpredictable. Slowing to a crawl can be as dangerous as joining a high-speed chain. The chain occurs when the motorist, driving blind and gambling that the road ahead is clear, is followed by other drivers whose vision is fixed on the taillights of the car ahead.

Maintaining Traction. Driving in conditions that reduce traction increases your stopping distance and the chance of skidding. Roads are especially hazardous when rain first begins to fall, because water, dust, and oil form a slippery film. Traction improves slightly as continuing rain "washes" the film from the road. In heavy rain, there is the danger of driving so fast that your tires are unable to push water away quickly enough, and they actually begin to ride on a film of water wedged between them and the road. The onset of this phenomenon, known as *hydroplaning,* depends mainly on your speed and the condition of your tires. The deeper the tread, the better the tires can shed water or allow it to escape before hydroplaning and a complete loss of traction occur.

Ice and snow can cause severe traction problems as well. If you must drive in such weather, get an immediate feel for the condition of the roads. Brake and accelerate gently until you discover how much traction you actually have. Steering should also be done smoothly; jerky driving can start a skid. Use extra care when leaving plowed and sanded major roads and turning onto side streets that may be icy.

All-season or snow tires are effective for improving traction, especially in fresh snow. It's best to have them mounted on all four wheels to increase their benefits when stopping, steering, and handling your car in icy conditions.

If you have to brake on ice or in snow in a car not equipped with antilock brakes, apply pedal pressure gently and try never to lock the brakes. Don't downshift for braking action; the sudden slowing of driving wheels can initiate a skid. On partially icy or snowy roads, scan conditions well ahead of your car and brake on dry patches of road.

If your car is equipped with traction control (for a sure grip when accelerating in slippery conditions), make sure the system is switched on.

Winterize Your Car. The other factor in the safety equation is the condition of your car. Proper car care is essential to avoid problems on the road, or to avoid the possibility of becoming stranded. In addition to the proper maintenance of your battery, lights, electrical system, ex-

SKID CONTROL

Knowing how to "catch" a skid is an essential driving skill. To regain control of the car, ease off the accelerator, then steer in the same direction as the skid (where the rear end of the car is heading). You want the front end of the car to catch up with the rear so the car will straighten itself out.

In the illustration below, the rear of the car is skidding left, so the front wheels should be turned left. If the rear slides right because you have "overcorrected" the skid, then turn the front wheels to the right. This technique works for both front- and rear-wheel-drive cars.

Sensing a skid and then correcting it can't be taught in driver education classes. If you want to become a truly expert driver, the ideal place to learn skid control is with an instructor in an advanced driving program.

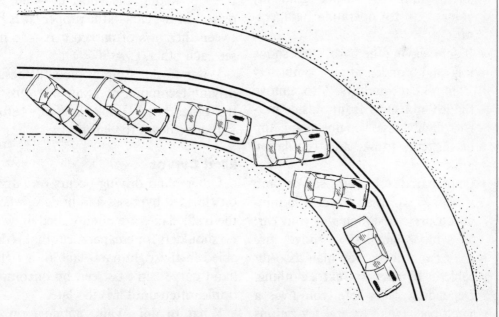

Knowing how to steer in a skid can keep you from "spinning out."

haust system, heating and cooling systems, windshield wipers and cleaning-fluid reservoir, brakes, and tires, other maintenance practices can minimize driving problems in winter. These are summarized in the following checklist:

- Fill your fuel tank frequently, never letting it get lower than half-full. You'll reduce condensation that forms in the unfilled part of the tank and avoid gas-line freeze-ups.
- Never warm up your car or let it idle in an enclosed area, such as an attached garage. Carbon monoxide can build up and seep into the car and into the house. To ensure proper engine lubrication, start the car only when you are ready to drive away, and then use low engine speeds until the engine gradually comes up to operating temperature.
- Before leaving the curb, clear snow, ice, and condensation completely from all car windows. Also remove the ice and snow from outside mirrors, light lenses, engine hood, top of the car, trunk, and ventilation grilles.
- Be prepared. A blizzard can entomb a stopped car in a snowdrift in minutes. Carry these items in your car: ice scraper, small snow shovel, tire chains and/or traction mats, booster cables, a blanket, and extra clothing. Depending on where you live, a small package of emergency rations may also be a good idea.

SPOTTING ACCIDENTS IN THE MAKING

Most accidents occur in the blink of an eye. There may be an instant of recognition but not enough time for the driver to act. However, preceding every sudden accident is a brief period of "setting up," as all the participants take their places. Then, if no one recognizes the pattern for disaster, the accident occurs. The following commonly occurring accidents are also the ones that often can be avoided.

Shopping Mall Shortcutters

Here is a simple, everyday accident: A driver cuts across a partially filled shopping mall parking lot, heedlessly crossing the parking-spot markings. The driver of the car taking the shortcut—and the drivers of the cars in the proper lanes between the rows of parked cars—do not see each other. *Crash!*

What to do: Employ your defensive driving technique of "watching out for the other guy." Look carefully before you drive down the lanes.

Blind Curves

Other blind driving occurs on curves on elevated bypasses and bridges, where the traffic lanes are often walled in, with no shoulders for escape. A car that is disabled in the right-hand lane of a right-hand curve can't be seen by oncoming traffic, often until it is too late.

What to do: Again, anticipation of such possibilities is the only way to avoid

ANTICIPATING UNPLEASANT SURPRISES

Anticipating, being ready to defuse an accident situation, and cooperating with other drivers can save you from being involved in a collision. In the illustration below, the "uninvolved driver" is the only one who can remove the threat of a potential accident.

At the top of the illustration, the uninvolved driver being passed is the first to see the car entering from the side street. He or she must swerve quickly to the shoulder and hope the other drivers will steer clear of one another.

At the bottom, there are two "uninvolved" drivers, but the one making the turn should realize what's happening behind and act quickly to get around the turn. This removes the potential for a major accident involving perhaps four or more cars.

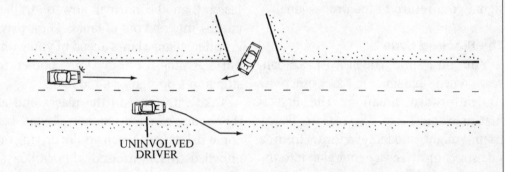

UNINVOLVED
DRIVER

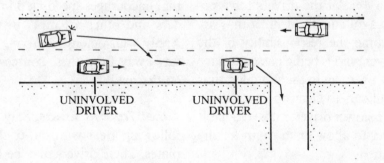

UNINVOLVED
DRIVER

UNINVOLVED
DRIVER

Always monitor the actions of other drivers, both ahead and behind. As the "uninvolved" driver, you may have to make escape maneuvers to avoid an accident.

a potential accident. When there is not enough time to stop, try to swerve around the obstacle. To take such evasive action means that you have to constantly monitor the traffic next to you and know where the gaps are at all times.

Any passing maneuver on a narrow road must be executed with great care, even if there appear to be no possible threats to the cars involved. Standard procedures are to signal your intention with your turn signals so the slower driver you're passing will be alerted, pass quickly on a clear stretch of road, and signal your return to the proper lane.

The Blocked Lane

You must anticipate at least two dangers when passing in an otherwise straightforward situation. The first is that a vehicle—or bicycle or pedestrian—might suddenly appear from a side street or driveway emerging into the oncoming lane that you are using for your pass.

What to do: All the drivers must cooperate to avoid an accident. It may actually become the responsibility of the slower driver who is being passed to save the day by swerving to the shoulder, thus allowing all cars to clear one another. If you are the slower driver, make it a habit to ease over to allow extra room for the passing car.

A second surprise situation might come from a driver farther down the road who is going in the same direction but slowing to make a right turn. The turning car will create a sudden block to the fast-moving driver who has just passed and now must get back into the lane because of oncoming traffic.

What to do: Again, the driver being passed may be the only one who can clear the road quickly enough to prevent an accident—by realizing what's happening behind and moving quickly with a right-hand turn, or even diving for the shoulder off the road.

Avoiding Risk-Takers

Usually, you can see them coming—drivers who are risk-takers, moving faster than the normal flow of traffic, cutting into and out of lanes. These drivers often change lanes ahead of you without signaling, or they don't bother to stop at a stop sign or a red light.

Take extra care in the places and at the hours when impatient drivers become risk-takers: when you're driving on crowded roads around the holidays, when commuting home at night, or when encountering stop-and-go traffic that encourages speeding on road shoulders and other attempts to cut ahead. Apply your defensive-driving skills, and stay away from these sources of danger on the road.

Other Trouble Areas. Stay alert when following a car with out-of-state license plates. These drivers may be looking for the right direction to take, and may make abrupt and unexpected stops and turns. In urban situations, try to avoid taxicabs without a fare—the driver may swerve across an entire avenue to pick up a passenger, or brake suddenly when hailed.

Outlaw Drivers

In an accident that occurred in 1993 in New York City, a driver ran a red light and broadsided another car. He had a suspended license, a record of nearly a dozen suspensions in less than three years, and was driving under the influ-ence of drugs. The driver of the other car was killed.

A growing number of drivers on the nation's highways have gone beyond being mere risk-takers. These are the outlaw drivers who continue to drive with suspended or revoked licenses. Often, they are under the influence of alcohol or drugs.

The accident described above was

LET 'EM PASS

Keeping impatient drivers boxed in behind your car only increases the chances that they'll involve *you* in an accident. If you're not in a hurry, appreciate the fact that other drivers may be intent on a destination. On narrow, no-passing roads with safe shoulders, pull over and wave them on.

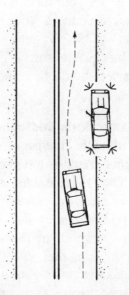

Let faster drivers pass; their impatience could create a dangerous situation.

clearly the fault of the impaired driver, who should not have been at the wheel of a car. Society has yet to find an effective way to keep these people off the road. That leaves your safety up to you. The more alert you are to other cars on the road, the better your chances of avoiding outlaw drivers.

HANDLING TROUBLE ON THE ROAD

A flat tire or a mechanical breakdown can put you in harm's way. If you park on the side of a busy highway, you may be hit by a passing car.

The average driver approaching your car at 60 mph needs as much as 200 feet to make a full stop, even more if the driver doesn't see your hazard flashers. If a hill or curve conceals your presence, the margin of safety may be even smaller. Thus, some sort of auxiliary warning device should be standard gear in every car.

Triangle Reflectors: Best Choice

Compared with emergency flares or warning lights, triangles have several advantages: They're reusable, and they don't require electrical power. You can place them hundreds of feet from the car. And they can sit in the trunk for years without losing their effectiveness.

To be effective at night, a triangle must be placed directly facing the traffic flow. Turn it more than a few degrees from that position and its visibility drops sharply.

You should have *at least three* triangles on hand so you can position them to guide other drivers safely around your vehicle.

Fusée Flares: Bright in Fog

Like triangle reflectors, flares can be placed as far from the car as necessary, and they don't require electrical power. These powder-filled tubes produce a small, bright red flame when they're struck like a match.

Flares do have an edge in heavy fog: They create a large red cloud effect. But though widely used, flares have a number of drawbacks:

- Flares don't command attention as well as triangles do in most weather conditions. Their light comes from one small source and isn't very conspicuous at a distance. The light could be mistaken for a taillight.
- A flare's light may not last until help arrives.
- Flares produce gagging fumes and smoke, and pose a fire hazard near dry brush or combustible materials.
- Flares can become damp and useless with time and should be replaced every three years.

Some flares have a wire stand that keeps the burning end off the ground. Others stand vertically when you push a spike into the ground. Spiked flares won't tip over, but they can be all but impossible to drive into concrete or asphalt. If you can't drive a flare into the ground, you'll have to lay it on its side. It will lose some of its visibility that way, and it may roll away. Even if you do manage to plant a spiked flare, it could flatten another car's tire if you don't remove the spike when you leave.

Flashing Lights: None Too Bright

These lights, which typically mount magnetically on the car roof, resemble the flasher on an emergency vehicle. They draw power from the car's cigarette-lighter socket, so they won't work when the problem is battery trouble.

Up close, the flashes emanating from these lights may seem bright enough. But from a couple of hundred feet away, even the better lights may be no more visible than the car's own emergency flashers.

Flashlights: Dim Bulbs

Add a couple of blinking bulbs to a flashlight, put a word like "hazard" on the package, and you have a product that might almost pass as a roadside emergency signal. Don't be taken in, though. These devices provide virtually no light from a distance. A flashlight can be valuable for making repairs in an emergency but not as a way to warn motorists.

EMERGENCY GEAR: A BASIC LIST

Something as minor as a shard of glass can disable a car without warning. If you don't have a cellular phone on board and so can't call for help immediately, you should carry other equipment to keep a brief delay from becoming a major interruption. The following list, by no means exhaustive, should serve as a rough guide. All the equipment is readily available at auto parts shops, hardware stores, and pharmacies.

Essentials

No car should be without a *first-aid kit,* which should include a variety of bandages. *Consumer Reports* found that of two Johnson & Johnson kits available, First Aid Kit 8155 (about $15 at most pharmacies) was better stocked than one targeted for use in a car.

The American Red Cross also sells a well-stocked first-aid kit for $30. Contact your local Red Cross chapter for ordering information.

A flat tire can be one of the simplest things to fix, provided you have a *lug wrench* and a working *jack* to make the change. Be sure the spare is ready for service: Check its pressure when you check the other tires.

If the battery conks out, *booster cables* enable a passing motorist to give you a jump start (see box below). If you drive in a cold climate, a hefty four- or six-gauge set of cables is recommended. For added reach, get a 16-foot version.

Other essentials include a *flashlight* and *spare change* for telephone calls. You might also want to carry a *white towel* or *pillowcase;* it can protect clothing if you have to crawl under the car, and it can serve as a warning flag.

JUMP-STARTING BASICS

Booster cables are easy to use, but proceed with caution. Never connect booster cables to a frozen battery, and don't smoke or hold an open flame near the battery—it might explode.

A *cross-connection* (linking one battery's positive terminal to the other's negative terminal and vice versa) may damage the alternators and expensive electronic equipment of both cars. The improper hookup will produce a shower of sparks. The battery may explode and spatter sulfuric acid.

When you're ready to jump-start a car, turn off the ignition and all electrical accessories in both cars. Make sure the cars are not touching. (On some late-model cars, you should also disconnect the electrical cable on the negative terminal to further protect the car's electronics. Check your owner's manual.)

Take out your booster cables, and hook the bright-colored clamps to each car's positive battery terminals (marked +, P, or Pos). Attach the cable to the disabled car first, then to the healthy car. Clip the black clamps to any unpainted part of each car's engine block or chassis—at least a foot from each battery. This time, connect the cable to the healthy car first. That will keep sparks away from the battery, minimizing the chance of an explosion.

Start the healthy car, and rev the engine a little. Then try to start the other car. If it starts, undo the clamps in reverse order and you should be on your way. If the jump start doesn't work, undo the cables and look elsewhere for the problem.

Basic Tools

You may not be handy with tools, but a passing Good Samaritan may be. Keep these tools in a small pouch or tackle box in the trunk: *pliers, screwdrivers* (both flat and Phillips head), *open-end wrenches, electrical tape* and *duct tape,* a *wire hanger,* and a *pocketknife.*

Extra Security

If you're willing to go the extra mile—possibly on foot—carry an empty *red container* specifically designed to hold gasoline, and bring along a siphon. Be sure the container is completely empty after you use it; air it out for a few min-utes, then cap it before you put it back in the trunk. When you get home, air the container outdoors until the gasoline fumes have dissipated.

A blown fuse can disable taillights or even prevent your car from running. Keep a few *replacement fuses* in the glove compartment. Check the car owner's manual for the size of fuses you need and the location of the fuse box.

You may never need to use a *fire extinguisher,* but you may want to keep one on board for an added sense of security. Be sure you buy one with an Underwriters Laboratories rating of at least 1A,10B,C. (These letters and numbers,

HOW TO STOP A RUNAWAY CAR

A car out of control can cause extensive damage and injury. Every driver should know how to prevent such a disaster.

Imagine, while you are driving, that your car suddenly races ahead of its own volition. The following steps can help you to bring it to a safe halt:

1. *Shift gears.* A racing engine cannot drive a car with an automatic transmission if the gearshift is moved to Neutral. In a car with manual transmission, depress the clutch pedal, effectively disconnecting the engine from the wheels.
2. *Apply the brakes.* Even a racing engine, whether caused by a stuck accelerator pedal, a mechanical defect, or an inadvertent step on the accelerator, cannot overpower the brakes. If, in a normal driving situation, you have applied the brakes and they seem to have failed, pump the brake pedal rapidly to build up hydraulic pressure (or follow the next step).
3. *Use the hand brake.* The hand brake is not as effective as the car's hydraulic brakes. But you should apply the hand brake if you have experienced complete brake failure and can't stop the car. With a hand brake, pull the handle up without "setting" it, so you can ease it off if the car begins to skid.

Faced with such a frightening situation, you may instinctively turn off the ignition. Generally, that's not recommended, because a dead engine has no power to assist the steering and brakes. Moreover, when the key is turned to the Park position, your steering wheel will lock, depriving you of any steering control whatsoever.

---

standard coding on fire extinguishers, denote a unit that can handle small fires of all types.)

BEFORE AND AFTER YOU DRIVE: PROTECT YOUR CAR

Many claims are filed with insurers not because of high-speed highway accidents but because of incidents occurring in driveways and parking lots. Such accidents are often caused by a failure to take simple precautions, like securing loose baggage before driving off.

Get in the habit of checking your car *before* you drive away, and taking extra care when parking it.

Give Your Car a Walkaround

Many people make a habit of walking around their car before getting in—whether it's parked in their driveway or on the street. Visibility from the driver's seat is limited, and sometimes pets, children's toys, or even the children themselves escape a driver's notice. Driveway tragedies occur every year simply because someone was eager to get going.

A walkaround before driving off also

affords a safety check of lenses, lights, and tires. Faulty brakes may also be caught, if you spot hydraulic fluid on the garage floor or in the driveway. In fact, checking the garage floor should become a habit, as you may pick up on other car problems, such as engine-oil or transmission-fluid leaks.

Once in the car, move slowly, especially in a driveway where something could be under your wheels. By driving slowly, you'll hear the sound of trouble, perhaps before much damage is done. In newer cars with automatic transmission interlocks, your foot must be on the brake to shift into gear. Take advantage of this arrangement and ease off the brakes slowly to start moving.

Park Out of Harm's Way

Smart car owners make it a habit to glance back at their car whenever and wherever they park and leave it. If all drivers did that, there would be fewer dead batteries from headlights left on by mistake. Perhaps other mishaps could be avoided, too. You may also have second thoughts about how the car is parked, whether the wheels are turned against the curb if the car is on a hill, whether the car is parked in a well-lit area to avoid a break-in or theft, and so on.

Thefts and Break-ins

When you park your car—anywhere—take certain antitheft precautions:

- Park in a well-lit, traveled area.
- Always lock your car.

- Leave nothing of value in the interior of the car or in the trunk.
- Do not leave your registration or other important documents in the glove compartment.
- Remember to activate the antitheft alarm or device, if there is one.

In many urban areas, even the usual precautions against theft and vandalism may not be sufficient. That's why alert city drivers who must park on the street will empty their glove compartments and leave them open, and fold rear seats, if so equipped, to show there's nothing in the trunk. If you have a removable radio, remember to take it out—but *don't* put it in the trunk.

Carjacking

Most car thefts involve unattended vehicles. But increasing incidents of *carjacking*—the commandeering of an auto by armed assailants—pose a new threat to drivers. A carjacking can occur at a parking garage, shopping center, gas station, traffic stop, and even on the road after deliberately staged minor accidents. The best advice, if confronted and trapped, is to simply hand over the keys and get out.

Avoid this type of opportunistic and violent crime by not driving in known high-crime areas, keeping doors locked and windows up, and choosing parking spots that are well lit and well traveled. Be alert when stopping for any reason, such as at a traffic light; leave enough room between you and the car ahead to pull away if necessary.

CAN YOU STOP A CAR THIEF?

An unprotected car is an easy mark for a properly equipped professional, who can unlock a door in less than a minute. Even an amateur using crude tools wouldn't need much time.

Car thieves want to work quickly and furtively, so the main goals of car alarms and other security devices are to scare thieves away or challenge them with a time-consuming task. In theory, a warning decal, blinking dashboard display, or some more obvious device warns thieves that your car won't be an easy mark. They may have to spend time disabling the protection you have installed—and they may set off flashing lights or a wailing siren in the process. Thieves willing to take those chances may gain entry to a car only to find that it can't be driven away easily; some security systems disable the engine.

SECURITY ALARMS: RECOMMENDED FEATURES

The more forms of resistance an alarm system presents, the more likely it is to foil a break-in. Some of the recommended features of an alarm system are the siren, engine disabler, intrusion sensors, hood and trunk protector, and remote panic alarm and door lock.

Siren. It should sound long enough to attract attention, but not so long that a false alarm disturbs the peace. Several cycles of a minute or two each should be adequate. In addition to sheer volume, a siren can call attention to itself by cycling through several unique sounds. Having the parking lights or headlights flash at the same time the siren sounds is another attention-getter.

Engine disabler. This important feature prevents the thief from starting the car. Most manufacturers recommend you set up the system to disable the starter. But that would be an indication to a thief of the presence of a security system, increasing the chances of its being found and bypassed. Disabling the ignition system is more effective, because it doesn't advertise the presence of the security system or its location. But doing so leaves a small risk that the disabler could malfunction while you're driving and cause the engine to stall.

Intrusion sensors. The more sensors the better. A sensor should protect all parts of the car equally. It should be designed so you can easily vary its sensitivity by adjusting a screw or a stem. Types of sensors include shock sensors, which detect a sharp blow to the vehicle's body; motion detectors, which react to jacking, swaying, or bouncing motions; and glass-breakage sensors, which respond if someone tampers with or breaks any of the car's glass.

Hood and trunk protection. Models that monitor electrical usage help protect doors, hood, and trunk. For instance, the alarm sounds if someone opens the door, and an interior light goes on. If the car lacks lights under the hood or in the trunk, the alarm system should come with a set of switches to protect hood and trunk.

Remote panic alarm. Standard on most systems, this allows you to trigger the alarm with the remote control if you see someone trying to break into the car or notice a suspicious person approaching while you're in the car.

Remote door lock. This is a useful feature for cars with power locks. When you arm the system, it automatically locks the doors and unlocks them when disarmed.

Convenience. This is important to the ultimate success of any alarm system. For instance, a remote control that operates from a long distance might let you control the system from your living room or set off the panic alarm at a safe distance from the car. Other handy features include an emergency override to disarm the alarm if the remote is missing or out of order; a valet switch (on passively armed models) to turn the system off when you hand the car over to a parking attendant; a dashboard display that tells you if the alarm was triggered while you were away; and well-written operating instructions.

Many auto security systems on the market are sold by specialized auto security shops or car-alarm dealers and are professionally installed. Choose an installer with care. Skill levels and fees vary considerably from one shop to another. People who prefer to install their own systems may have a hard time installing a sophisticated system, which generally requires a high level of skill. If you've never drilled through sheet metal or poked around under the dashboard, installing an alarm is likely to be frustrating and perhaps damaging to your car.

Clubs. Bar locks, or clubs, try to stop a thief by shackling a car's steering wheel, brake, or shifter. Perhaps the best-known bar lock is The Club (about $60). The hardened-steel bar itself is too hard to cut, but the steering wheel is easily sliced through, and the lock can be slipped off like a ring from the finger. While it may be a deterrent to a casual thief, you shouldn't depend solely on The Club or any other steering-wheel locks.

If your car is bumped from behind, especially in a deserted area, do *not* get out of the car. Instead, signal the other driver to follow you to a police station or some other safe place. Be alert when arriving home as well; someone may have followed you. Signal your arrival to those at home with a tap of your horn.

THE OLDER DRIVER

The effects of aging on driving skills often go unrecognized, especially for healthy people enjoying their later years. These effects may include slowed reaction time; lessened perception and ability to judge speed; diminished vision, especially peripheral and night vision; sensitivity to glare; impaired hearing, especially in the higher frequencies; and sometimes a loss of physical agility.

Highway statistics tell the story: Motor vehicle death rates are higher for elderly people than for younger adults. According to the Insurance Institute for Highway Safety (IIHS), elderly drivers have higher fatal crash rates (per mile driven) than drivers in other age groups, except teenagers. Moving violations statistics also indicate that elderly drivers are more likely than younger ones to be cited for failure to yield, for improper turns, and for running stop signs and red lights.

These unpleasant statistics don't belie the fact that older drivers have the advantages of experience, patience, and judgment. And no one is saying that the elderly have no place on the road. Clearly, however, elderly motorists must concentrate harder to drive as safely as they did during their middle years.

Improving Driving Techniques

Most driving limitations associated with aging can be compensated for, but the use of medications is a special case. Always consult with your physician about any medication you must take that might affect your ability to drive safely.

Make sure that you feel fit and alert before driving. Check your seating position, observe distances, be especially wary of left turns, and use traffic controls to your advantage.

Keeping Fit and Alert. Exercise maintains mobility and physical flexibility. It also fights fatigue and depression, which can cause distraction and carelessness at the wheel. Adequate rest is important before driving long distances, and frequent rest stops should be made when on the road.

Good drivers of any age, many of them professionals, say that strict concentration on their driving usually helps to prevent them from ever nodding off at the wheel; they pull over to the side of the road for a nap before they ever get to the point of letting their lids close over their eyes while driving.

If your concentration is not that disciplined, you'll have to develop your own system for staying awake while driving, especially if you can't or won't pull over to rest. Some drivers play the radio and sing along with the music. Some chew gum, drink coffee, or leave the window open to get as much fresh air as possible. Do whatever works for you.

Some commercial gimmicks have been developed to wake nodding drivers, but these have had limited success. One device, worn on a hat, detects when your head varies from the vertical position and sets off a buzzer. Another measures how often the driver makes corrections to the steering wheel, which is quite often for normal, alert driving. If all steering-wheel movements stop, a loud buzzer sounds to alert the driver.

Good Posture. People may shrink several inches by the time they've reached their mid-seventies. This alteration in height can affect your posture, and you have to remember to compensate for it. It's also dangerous to operate a car if you're sitting so low that you don't have proper visibility or control.

If the car's usual adjustments don't raise the seat enough and if a mechanic can't raise it, then install some firm supports and pillows that will position you properly. Generally, the top of your shoulders should be as high as the top of the steering wheel. (Use the tilt and telescoping controls if your steering wheel is so equipped.) At the same time, check that you can quickly and easily operate all foot controls, and make sure that the head restraint is set for your height. Finally, adjust all mirrors for maximum visibility.

Test Your Reflexes. Reaction time is important. Every fraction of a second lost in reaction time while driving means you are going to travel that much farther toward a dangerous situation before being able to brake or swerve.

As we age, we cannot react as quickly to emergencies as when we were younger. We also cannot perceive dangers as readily. Once you reach this awareness, you'll be ready to work to compensate for the loss. (To test your reaction time, take the test on page 95.)

Keep Your Distance. The following distances between cars become tailgating at different points for different people. Now, the old system of judging car lengths and checking your speedometer has given way to a technique that doesn't require estimating distances or taking your eyes off the road. The new method works simply by counting.

The *three-second rule for following* is

FOLLOWING-DISTANCE RULE

On dry roads, to allow enough room between your car and the car ahead, use this counting technique.

As the rear of the car ahead passes a checkpoint (such as a sign, overpass, or some other roadway marker), begin to count: 1,001, 1,002, and so on. Stop counting when the front of your car arrives at that checkpoint. If it takes less than two seconds for you to get there, you're following too closely. If you take two seconds or more to get to the checkpoint, you're following at a safe distance. A three-second interval, however, is best.

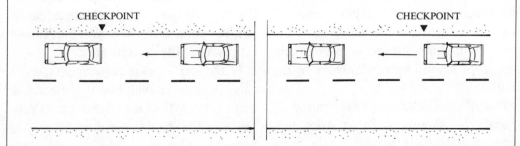

Counting seconds after a checkpoint can help you establish a safe following distance.

part of the 55 Alive/Mature Driving courses offered by the American Association of Retired People (AARP). Here, the following distance is given in seconds and is automatically adjusted for speed, and a three-second following distance is recommended at all speeds (see box below). The rule is meant to be applied while driving on dry pavement, and it should be practiced until it becomes a habit. On wet and slippery roads, the following distance should be increased.

Use Traffic Signals Wisely. Older drivers—and, in fact, drivers of all ages—are well advised to forgo the shortest route to their destinations if it involves a left turn from a side street onto a busy major highway with a yield or stop sign as the only traffic control. Because of the heavy volume of traffic, a left turn across busy lanes can be almost impossible to make. Drive to the next block or go even farther if necessary to take advantage of a signal that will give you a safer "green" time for entering the highway.

Even a traffic light is no guarantee of safe passage, however. Treat the green light as a flashing yellow, which means proceed with caution. Look left and right for any drivers in the cross traffic who are deliberately or inadvertently running the light.

Too Old to Drive?

Last year, Aunt Hattie sold her car. It was something she did reluctantly, but she knew it was time to stop driving. Aunt Hattie was 98 years old this year. She's in wonderful health—mentally and physically—but she was smart enough to realize that everyone reaches a point when compensating for age just doesn't work anymore, especially when driving a car.

Unfortunately, many older drivers refuse to recognize when their strength, vision, hearing, concentration, and memory are not what they once were. They may insist on driving when they shouldn't be on the road at all.

Driving behavior can reveal driving problems. Drivers find it difficult to evaluate their own driving, so they should ask a friend to be alert to their driving habits and to be frank about their limitations. Some disquieting signs include:

- *Hesitation.* How long does it take the driver to get moving after the light changes to green? Too long a pause may indicate a slowed reaction time, daydreaming, or memory lapses. Hesitation may also be present when merging, in making too wide a turn, and in driving too slowly for traffic conditions.
- *Awareness.* Is the driver unmoving and rigid at the wheel? Eyes should be moving constantly, checking up and down the road ahead and in blind spots left and right. Mirrors also should be used continually. Elderly drivers who appear nervous or frightened at the wheel are likely to have lost their edge.
- *Braking.* In compensating for slowed reaction time, older drivers may "ride" the brakes, leaving their foot on the brake pedal almost con-

SAFE DRIVING TIPS FOR OLDER PEOPLE

About 90 percent of driving decisions are based on information received through the eyes. Therefore, a change in vision can have a profound effect on driving ability. Being aware of the changes that occur with age, and taking them into account while driving, can help you prevent accidents. The following tips from the American Optometric Association are good, commonsense recommendations for drivers of all ages, but especially for those over 50.

- *Have regular eye examinations to determine day and night vision capabilities.* If corrective lenses are prescribed, choose frames that do not block peripheral vision. You may be able to pass the eye test for a driver's license without corrective lenses, but it may be safer to wear them, especially for night driving. Take time to adjust to the lenses before attempting to drive. On bright days, wear sunglasses; gray lenses are usually recommended.
- *Drive at speeds and on roads where you feel comfortable.* Keep pace with the traffic flow, driving neither too fast nor too slowly. Make use of mirrors, but be aware of blind spots. If you have difficulty seeing over the dashboard, sit on a pillow. Move your head as well as your eyes to keep track of traffic all around you. Stiffness in the neck combined with decreased peripheral vision will limit your line of sight. Be particularly careful when backing out. Convex mirrors placed opposite blind driveways on hills or curves are helpful in letting you see oncoming traffic.
- *Don't wear sunglasses or tinted lenses while driving at night.* If your night vision is impaired, limit your driving to well-lit, familiar roads. Make sure the headlights and taillights are working. Dusk and daybreak actually provide the most troublesome light conditions for driving; if possible, avoid driving at these times.
- *Do not smoke or eat while driving.* It can distract your attention from the road and impede vision if smoke gets into your eyes. Nicotine also interferes with night vision. If you are taking any prescription or nonprescription medication, ask your doctor or pharmacist or read the label carefully to determine driving recommendations. And, of course, *never* drink and drive.

stantly. Riding the brakes is a sure sign that an older driver is too hesitant and fearful to drive.

Limited Licenses

To protect older drivers and to keep them from harming others, some states have introduced "graded licenses." In this system, frequent driving tests may be required at any time at the request of family or physicians. Drivers may face restrictions on their driving, depending on how they do in the tests.

A limited license allows older drivers to maintain their independence by driving locally. Such drivers are not allowed to drive in fast-moving traffic on highways, expressways, or in crowded urban areas.

It is unlikely that any state will impose an age cutoff for driving. But with the expected increase in the older population, more states will have to address the issue of aging and driving, perhaps by initiating periodic testing.

HOW TO BECOME A PREFERRED DRIVER

Four rules of good driving can almost guarantee your safety on the road and, as an added benefit, can put you into the Preferred Driver insurance category. The "four Cs" of driving behavior are

- Concentration
- Cooperation
- Communication
- Courtesy

Concentration while driving is essential: Don't allow yourself to be distracted. Keep your eyes on the road (and on your mirrors), and be aware of the traffic around you.

Cooperation means you appreciate the fact that you're not the only driver on the road.

Communication is another aspect of cooperation. You are not isolated in your car but part of the general traffic flow around you. If you see a potential accident, you must have concern for the drivers around you.

Courtesy means a wave to other drivers when they signal to you to go ahead, or when they slow or stop to allow you to leave a side street. And a wave of apology if you make a move that was perhaps a bit too abrupt can help allay hostility.

Driving skillfully, with a sense of social responsibility, makes roads safer and driving a more enjoyable activity.

Appendix A

CONSUMER REPORTS RATINGS OF AUTO INSURANCE COMPANIES

Price may be foremost in shopping for auto insurance, but service becomes crucial if you're ever in an accident and need to file a claim. In fact, promptness in handling claims emerged as the single most significant factor in customer satisfaction, according to a 1991 survey of 63,000 *Consumer Reports* readers.

The Ratings of insurers in the following chart indicate how well they have satisfied their customers, specifically *Consumer Reports* subscribers. Areas covered include claims problems, non-claims problems, delayed payments, drop rate, and where the companies sell their policies. The Comments column supplies information specific to that particular insurer.

The highest-rated carrier, Amica Mutual Insurance Company, completely satisfied 79 percent of its clients, according to this survey. Amica, which sells its policies exclusively by telephone, was also among the top-rated insurers in past *Consumer Reports* surveys of auto insurance companies. Unfortunately, it's not easy to get coverage from Amica, because the company accepts applications only from people who have been referred to it by current customers. Several of the other top-rated insurers also limit their customer base to specific demographic or professional groups. To avoid disappointment, check the Comments column of the Ratings for that information.

Ratings of auto insurance

Better ← → Worse

As published in the August 1992 issue of *Consumer Reports*

Listed in order of overall reader satisfaction with claims handling, based on responses to a 1991 Annual Questionnaire. More than 63,000 readers told Consumers Union about their experiences with claims they had filed in the previous three years. Each of the 49 companies listed here was evaluated by at least 200 respondents. These results reflect the experiences of *Consumer Reports* readers, not necessarily the experience of all auto-insurance policyholders.

Overall score. The degree of satisfaction with a company. If all respondents were completely satisfied, the company would have scored 100. If all were completely dissatisfied, the company would have scored 0. Differences of less than five points between companies are not meaningful. The median score was 85.

Levels of satisfaction. The percentage of respondents who said they were completely satisfied; very or fairly well satisfied; and somewhat, very, or completely dissat-

isfied. These percentages are summarized in the Overall score, explained above.

Claims problems. Better companies drew fewer complaints about one or more of the following: agent or company delays in handling the claim, difficulty reaching the right company representative, discourteous treatment, complicated procedures, disagreement over who was at fault, disagreement over the dollar value of damages, disagreement over what the policy covered, and delay in payment. For the best compa-

Company	Overall score	Levels of satisfaction	Claims problems	Nonclaims problems	Delayed payments	Drop rate	Where sold	Comments
Amica Mutual Insurance	94		◉	◉	5%	◑	—	A,B
Cincinnati Insurance	93		◉	◑	3	○	a,b,c	—
United Services Automobile Assn.	93		◑	◉	6	◑	—	A,B,C
PEMCO Mutual Insurance	92		◉	○	4	◑	d	D
USAA Casualty Insurance	91		◑	◉	7	◑	—	A,B,C
National General Insurance	91		◑	○	7	○	—	B,E
Hartford Underwriters Insurance	90		◑	○	9	◑	—	F
Auto-Owners Insurance	89		○	○	8	○	a,b,c	—
New Jersey Manufacturers Insurance	89		◑	◉	9	◑	e,f	A,B,G
Citizens Insurance Co. of America	89		◑	○	4	○	g,h	E
Erie Insurance Exchange	88		◑	○	9	○	a,c,f	—
Erie Insurance Co.	87		◑	○	5	○	a,c,f	—
Nationwide Mutual Fire Insurance	87		○	○	8	○	—	H
State Farm Mutual Automobile Insurance	87		○	○	7	◑	—	I
Country Mutual Insurance	86		○	○	5	○	a,i	A,H
American Family Mutual Insurance	86		○	○	5	○	a,b	—
West American Insurance	86		○	○	9	○	—	—
Colonial Penn Insurance	86		○	◑	12	○	—	B
Hartford Accident & Indemnity	86		○	○	10	○	—	—
American States Insurance	86		○	◉	7	◑	—	—
Transamerica Insurance	86		○	○	12	○	—	—
Hartford Insurance Co. of the Midwest	85		○	○	11	◑	—	F
State Automobile Mutual Insurance	85		○	○	8	○	a,c	—
State Farm Fire & Casualty Insurance	85		○	○	8	○	—	—
Illinois Farmers Insurance	85		○	○	5	◑	—	—

Key to Where sold
 a–Midwest
 b–Southwest
 c–Southeast
 d–Washington
 e–New Jersey
 f–Pennsylvania
 g–Michigan
 h–Indiana
 i–West
 j–California
 k–Nevada
 l–Kansas

m–Texas and North Carolina
n–Massachusetts

Key to Comments
 A–May offer annual dividend.
 B–Generally sold by mail or telephone.
 C–Sold only to current or retired military officers or their families.
 D–Subsidiary sells only to educators.
 E–Sold mainly to members of some associations or employees of some companies.
 F–In most states, sold only to American Association of Retired Persons members.

G–Sold only to people whose employers are members of the New Jersey Business and Industry Association. Also sold to state employees.
H–In one or more states, sold only to farm bureau members.
 I–Membership fee may be charged.
J–Sold only to government employees and members of the military.
K–Sold only to auto club members.
L–Name changed in 1990 to Metropolitan Property & Casualty Insurance Co.
M–Insures mainly high-risk drivers.

nies, no more than 8.7 percent of respondents complained about claims problems; for the worst, 26.9 percent or more complained.

Nonclaims problems. Better companies had fewer complaints about the following perceived problems: excessive rate increases, poor service in changing policy information or coverage, difficulty contacting company representatives, unclear explanation of coverage, and late or incorrect billing. The best companies had 9.7 percent or fewer complaints; the worst companies had 33 percent or more complaints.

Delayed payments. The percentage of readers who said they received a settlement from their insurer more than 30 days after filing a claim. For the average insurer, 9.2 percent of respondents said they had been paid more than 30 days after filing their claim.

Drop rate. Companies that canceled or refused to renew 0.5 percent or fewer of our respondents' policies scored better than average. Companies that dropped 2 percent or more of them scored worse than average. Reasons cited, according to our readers: too many claims; too many traffic-law violations; other, unspecified reasons; or no reasons given by the company. The drop rate here does not include policies dropped because the insurer left the state, stopped doing business with a respondent's agent, or because the respondent didn't pay the premium.

Where sold. Indicates companies that sell primarily in one state or one part of the country. A dash indicates company sells nationally.

Company	Overall score	Levels of satisfaction	Claims problems	Nonclaims problems	Delayed payments	Drop rate	Where sold	Comments
Nationwide Mutual Insurance	85		○	○	8	○	—	—
Liberty Mutual Fire Insurance	84		○	○	10	○	—	—
Royal Insurance Co. of America	84		○	○	12	◑	—	—
Government Employees Insurance	84		○	○	9	○	—	A,B,J
Horace Mann Insurance	84		○	●	10	◑	—	—
GEICO General Insurance	84		○	○	10	◑	—	A,B
Auto Club Insurance Assn. (Michigan)	83		○	●	7	◑	g	A,K
SAFECO Insurance Co. of America	83		○	○	9	○	—	—
California State Automobile Assn.	83		○	○	11	◑	j,k	A,K
United States Fidelity & Guaranty	83		○	○	11	◑	—	—
Allstate Insurance	82		○	◑	9	○	—	—
Continental Insurance	82		○	○	10	○	—	—
Farmers Insurance Co. (Kansas)	82		○	○	8	○	I	—
Farmers Insurance Exchange	82		◑	◑	11	○	—	—
Liberty Mutual Insurance	82		◑	○	10	○	m	—
Aetna Casualty & Surety	81		◑	◑	13	◑	—	—
Travelers Indemnity	80		◑	◑	11	○	—	—
Prudential Property & Casualty Insurance	80		◑	●	13	◑	—	—
20th Century Insurance	79		●	○	18	○	j	B
General Accident Insurance Co. of America	79		●	○	13	○	—	—
Metropolitan Property & Liability Insurance	79		◑	◑	12	○	—	L
Allstate Indemnity	79		◑	●	13	○	—	I,M
Hanover Insurance	77		●	○	12	○	—	—
Commerce Insurance	75		●	●	18	○	n	—

Appendix B

—

STATE INSURANCE DEPARTMENTS

State insurance departments are listed below, along with telephone numbers that consumers can call with questions, comments, or complaints. Toll-free "800" numbers are available only for in-state calls.

ALABAMA
Commissioner of Insurance
135 South Union Street
Montgomery, AL 36130-3351
Tel. 205-269-3591 or 205-269-3595

ALASKA
Director of Insurance
P.O. Box 110805
Juneau, AK 99811-0805
Tel. 907-465-2515
For consumer complaints: 800 E.
   Dimond Boulevard, Suite 3-560,
   Anchorage, AK 99515-2045
   Tel: 907-349-1230

ARIZONA
Director of Insurance
3030 North Third Street, Suite 1100
Phoenix, AZ 85012
Tel. 602-255-5400 or 800-325-2548

ARKANSAS
Insurance Commissioner
1123 South University, Suite 400
University Tower Building
Little Rock, AR 72204-1699
Tel. 501-686-2900
Consumer services: 501-686-2945 or
   800-852-5494

CALIFORNIA
Commissioner of Insurance
770 L Street, Suite 1120
Sacramento, CA 95814
Tel. 916-445-5544 or 800-927-HELP

COLORADO
Commissioner of Insurance
1560 Broadway, Suite 850
Denver, CO 80202
Tel. 303-894-7499

CONNECTICUT
Insurance Commissioner
P.O. Box 816
Hartford, CT 06142-0816
Tel. 203-297-3900

DELAWARE
Insurance Commissioner
The Rodney Building
841 Silver Lake Boulevard
Dover, DE 19901
Tel. 302-739-4251 or 800-282-8611

DISTRICT OF COLUMBIA
Superintendent of Insurance
613 G Street, NW
Sixth Floor
Washington, DC 20013-7200
Tel. 202-727-8000 or 202-727-7434

FLORIDA
Insurance Commissioner
State Capitol
Plaza Level 11, 200 East Gaines St.
Tallahassee, FL 32399-0300
Tel. 904-922-3132 or 800-342-2762

GEORGIA
Insurance Commissioner
2 Martin Luther King Jr. Drive
Floyd Memorial Building
West Tower
Seventh Floor
Atlanta, GA 30334
Tel. 404-656-2056

HAWAII
Insurance Commissioner
P.O. Box 3614
Honolulu, HI 96811
Tel. 808-586-2790 or 800-468-4644

IDAHO
Director of Insurance
700 West State Street
J. R. Williams Building
Third Floor
Boise, ID 83720
Tel. 208-334-2250

ILLINOIS
Director of Insurance
320 West Washington Street
Fourth Floor
Springfield, IL 62767
Tel. 217-782-4515 or 217-782-7446

INDIANA
Commissioner of Insurance
311 West Washington Street
Suite 300
Indianapolis, IN 46204
Tel. 317-232-2385 or 800-622-4461

IOWA
Commissioner of Insurance
Lucas State Office Building
Sixth Floor
Des Moines, IA 50319
Tel. 515-281-5705

KANSAS
Commissioner of Insurance
420 South West Ninth Street
Topeka, KS 66612-1678
Tel. 913-296-3071 or 800-432-2484

KENTUCKY
Insurance Commissioner
229 West Main Street
P.O. Box 517
Frankfort, KY 40602
Tel. 502-564-3630

LOUISIANA
Commissioner of Insurance
P.O. Box 94214
Capitol Station
Baton Rouge, LA 70804-9214
Tel. 504-342-5900 or 800-259-5300

MAINE
Superintendent of Insurance
State House
Station 34
Augusta, ME 04333
Tel. 207-582-8707 or 800-300-5000

MARYLAND
Insurance Commissioner
501 St. Paul Place
Seventh Floor South
Baltimore, MD 21202
Tel. 410-333-6300

MASSACHUSETTS
Commissioner of Insurance
280 Friend Street
Boston, MA 02114
Tel. 617-727-3333 or 617-727-7189

MICHIGAN
Commissioner of Insurance
P.O. Box 30220
Lansing, MI 48909
Tel. 517-373-9273

MINNESOTA
Commissioner of Commerce
133 East Seventh Street
St. Paul, MN 55101
Tel. 612-296-6848 or 612-296-2488
   (enforcement office)

MISSISSIPPI
Commissioner of Insurance
1804 Walter Sillers Building
Jackson, MS 39201
or:
P.O. Box 79
Jackson, MS 39205
Tel. 601-359-3569 or 800-562-2957

MISSOURI
Director of Insurance
301 West High Street
P.O. Box 690
Jefferson City, MO 65102-0690
Tel. 314-751-2640 or 800-726-7390

MONTANA
Commissioner of Insurance
126 North Sanders
Mitchell Building, Room 270
Helena, MT 59601
or:
P.O. Box 4009
Helena, MT 59604
Tel. 406-444-2040 or 800-332-6148

NEBRASKA
Director of Insurance
941 O Street, Suite 400
Lincoln, NE 68508
Tel. 402-471-2201

NEVADA
Commissioner of Insurance
1665 Hot Springs Road, Suite 152
Capitol Complex
Carson City, NV 89710
Tel. 702-687-4270 or 800-992-0900,
    ext. 4270 (in Las Vegas, call ext.
    4009)

NEW HAMPSHIRE
Insurance Commissioner
169 Manchester Street
Concord, NH 03301
Tel. 603-271-2261 or 800-852-3416

NEW JERSEY
Commissioner of Insurance
20 West State Street, CN 329
Trenton, NJ 08625
Tel. 609-292-5317 or 800-446-SHOP

NEW MEXICO
Superintendent of Insurance
P.O. Drawer 1269
Santa Fe, NM 87504-1269
Tel. 505-827-4592

NEW YORK
Superintendent of Insurance
160 West Broadway
New York, NY 10013
Tel. 212-602-0203 or 800-342-3736

NORTH CAROLINA
Commissioner of Insurance
P.O. Box 26387
Raleigh, NC 27611
Tel. 919-733-2032 or 800-662-7777

NORTH DAKOTA
Commissioner of Insurance
Capitol Building, Fifth Floor
600 East Boulevard Ave.
Bismarck, ND 58505-0320
Tel. 701-224-2440 or 800-247-0560

OHIO
Director of Insurance
2100 Stella Court
Columbus, OH 43266-0566
Tel. 614-644-2658 or 800-686-1526

OKLAHOMA
Insurance Commissioner
P.O. Box 53408
Oklahoma City, OK 71352-3408
Tel. 405-521-2828 or 800-522-0071

OREGON
Insurance Commissioner
440-1 Labor and Industries Building
Salem, OR 97310-0765
Tel. 503-378-4271; Tel. 503-378-4636
    or 503-378-4484 (consumer
    advocate)

PENNSYLVANIA
Insurance Commissioner
1326 Strawberry Square
13th Floor
Harrisburg, PA 17120
Tel. 717-787-5173 or dial the consumer
    number in your area code: 717-787-
    2317; 215-560-2630; 412-565-5020;
    or 814-871-4466

RHODE ISLAND
Associate Director and Superintendent
    of Insurance
233 Richmond Street, Suite 233
Providence, RI 02903-4233
Tel. 401-277-2223

SOUTH CAROLINA
Chief Insurance Commissioner
1612 Marion Street
P.O. Box 100105
Columbia, SC 29202-3105
Tel. 803-737-6140 or 800-768-3467

SOUTH DAKOTA
Director of Insurance
500 East Capitol
Pierre, SD 57501
Tel. 605-773-3563

TENNESSEE
Commissioner of Insurance
500 James Robertson Parkway
Nashville, TN 37243-0600
Tel. 615-741-2241 or 800-342-8385

TEXAS
Commissioner of Insurance
333 Guadalupe
P.O. Box 149091
Austin, TX 78714-9091
Tel. 512-463-6515 or 800-252-3439

UTAH
Commissioner of Insurance
3110 State Office Building, Room 3110
Salt Lake City, UT 84114
Tel. 801-538-3800 or 800-439-3805

VERMONT
Commissioner of Banking, Securities,
    and Insurance
State Office Building
89 Main Street, Drawer 20
Montpelier, VT 05620-3101
Tel. 802-828-3301

VIRGINIA
Commissioner of Insurance
1300 East Main St.
Richmond, VA 23209
or:
P.O. Box 1157
Richmond, VA 23209
Tel. 804-371-9741 or 800-552-7945

WASHINGTON
Insurance Commissioner
Insurance Building
P.O. Box 40255
Olympia, WA 98504-0255
Tel. 206-753-7301 or -7300; 800-562-
   6900

WEST VIRGINIA
Insurance Commissioner
2019 Washington Street East
Charleston, WV 25305
Tel. 304-558-3394 or 800-642-9004

WISCONSIN
Commissioner of Insurance
121 East Wilson Street
Madison, WI 53702
or:
P.O. Box 7873
Madison, WI 53707
Tel. 608-266-0103 or 800-236-8517

WYOMING
Insurance Commissioner
Herschler Building
122 West 25th Street
Cheyenne, WY 82002
Tel. 307-777-7401 or 800-442-4333

Appendix C

—

SOURCES OF HELP

If you have a complaint or problem regarding your insurance company, the best place to start is with the agent or customer relations department of the insurer itself. Your problem may be a clerical mistake or a miscommunication that can be easily resolved. The next step is to complain to your state insurance department (see Appendix B). In many states, such departments have established facilities for resolving individual complaints. Some states—Texas, for example—have insurance advocates dedicated to resolving consumer insurance problems. In addition, some large cities—notably New York City—have consumer affairs departments with some expertise in insurance.

You might also consider talking to a local legislator about your case. The state bar association can supply names of attorneys if you believe your case warrants legal action.

The following national organizations offer consumer information (brochures, books, how-to articles) on insurance laws and coverage, but generally don't have the resources to solve individual problems.

Consumers Union
101 Truman Avenue
Yonkers, NY 10703-1057
914-378-2000

Publishes *Consumer Reports* magazine and books on numerous insurance issues.

Insurance Information Institute
110 William Street
New York, NY 10038
212-669-9200

Publishes numerous brochures and books on auto and homeowner's insurance. The organization's toll-free consumer Helpline is 800-942-4242. This industry-sponsored hot line can answer general questions about coverage and claims.

National Consumers League
815 15th Street, NW
Suite 928
Washington, DC 20005
202-639-8140
   Publishes consumer guides to insurance.

National Insurance Consumer
   Organization
121 North Payne Street
Alexandria, VA 22314
703-549-8050
   Publishes consumer guides to homeowner's and auto insurance.

Appendix D

—

INSURANCE COSTS FOR SPECIFIC CARS

The following chart can help you evaluate what it will cost, generally, to insure a particular make and model of car. Different models receive different insurance treatments because, in the view of insurance companies, they represent different levels of risk that there will be a damage claim. Sporty cars, for instance, usually generate more claims to an insurance company (either through damage or theft) than family cars, so they tend to cost more to insure. Some cars may sustain more damage, or more costly damage, in a collision than similar cars, so they are more expensive to repair—and insure.

Keep in mind, however, that many factors besides the model you choose can influence your auto insurance premium. They include your age, sex, and driving record, where you live, whether the car is used for commuting to work, what other drivers are in the family, and whether the car is equipped with antitheft devices. Moreover, insurance regulations differ from state to state, and in most states different insurance companies can charge different rates.

HOW TO USE THE CHART

The column labeled Insurance gives an idea, where available, of the relative cost of the collision and comprehensive portions of the car owner's auto insurance premium. These coverages can differ in price by 10, 20, or 30 percent between two cars in the same price class. These judgments are derived from a system developed by the Insurance Services Office (ISO), an insurance-industry organization. The evaluations are based on insurance claims experience with 1992 model cars, the latest year available as of this writing, but they should be broadly applicable to 1993 and 1994 cars as well.

CAR NAME	INSURANCE	CAR NAME	INSURANCE
Acura Integra	NA	Dodge Grand Caravan	Low
Acura Legend	Low	Dodge Intrepid	NA
Acura Vigor	Average	Dodge Neon	NA
Audi 90	NA	Dodge Shadow	Average
Audi 100	Low	Dodge Spirit	Low
BMW 3-Series	High	Dodge Stealth	High
BMW 5-Series	NA	Eagle Summit	NA
BMW 740	NA	Eagle Summit Wagon	NA
Buick Century	Low	Eagle Talon	High
Buick Le Sabre	Low	Eagle Vision	NA
Buick Park Avenue	Low	Ford Aerostar	Low
Buick Regal	Low	Ford Aspire	NA
Buick Roadmaster	Low	Ford Bronco	NA
Buick Skylark	Average	Ford Crown Victoria	Low
Cadillac Deville	NA	Ford Escort	Average
Cadillac Eldorado	NA	Ford Explorer	Low
Cadillac Fleetwood	NA	Ford Mustang	NA
Cadillac Seville	NA	Ford Probe	High
Chevrolet Astro	Low	Ford Taurus	Low
Chevrolet Blazer	Average	Ford Tempo	Average
Chevrolet Camaro	NA	Ford Thunderbird	Average
Chevrolet Caprice	Low	Geo Metro	High
Chevrolet Cavalier	Average	Geo Prizm	NA
Chevrolet Corsica	Average	Geo Tracker	High
Chevrolet Corvette	NA	GMC Jimmy	Average
Chevrolet Lumina	Low	GMC Safari	Low
Chevrolet Suburban	Average	GMC Suburban	Average
Chevrolet S-10 Blazer	Average	GMC Yukon	Average
Chrysler Concorde	NA	Honda Accord	NA
Chrysler LeBaron	NA	Honda Civic	Average
Chrysler LeBaron Convertible	Average	Honda Del Sol	NA
Chrysler New Yorker	NA	Honda Prelude	High
Chrysler New Yorker LHS	NA	Hyundai Elantra	Average
Chrysler Town and Country	Low	Hyundai Excel	High
Dodge Caravan	Low	Hyundai Scoupe	High
Dodge Colt	NA	Hyundai Sonata	NA
		Infiniti G20	Average
		Infiniti J30	NA

CAR NAME	INSURANCE	CAR NAME	INSURANCE
Infiniti Q45	Average	Mitsubishi Galant	NA
Isuzu Amigo	Average	Mitsubishi Mirage	NA
Isuzu Rodeo	Average	Mitsubishi Montero	Average
Isuzu Trooper	Average	Nissan 240 SX	NA
Jaguar XJ6	Average	Nissan 300ZX	Average
Jeep Cherokee	Average	Nissan Altima	NA
Jeep Grand Cherokee	NA	Nissan Maxima	NA
Jeep Wrangler	Average	Nissan Pathfinder	NA
Lexus ES300	Average	Nissan Quest	NA
Lexus GS300	NA	Nissan Sentra	High
Lexus LS400	Low	Oldsmobile 88 Royale	Low
Lexus SC400	Average	Oldsmobile 98 Regency	Low
Lincoln Continental	Average	Oldsmobile Achieva	Average
Lincoln Mark VIII	NA	Oldsmobile Bravada	Average
Lincoln Town Car	Low	Oldsmobile Cutlass Ciera	Low
Mazda 323	High	Oldsmobile Cutlass Supreme	Low
Mazda 626	Average	Oldsmobile Silhouette	Low
Mazda 929	Average	Plymouth Acclaim	Low
Mazda MPV	Average	Plymouth Colt	NA
Mazda MX-3	Average	Plymouth Colt Vista	Average
Mazda MX-5 Miata	Average	Plymouth Grand Voyager	Low
Mazda MX-6	High	Plymouth Laser	NA
Mazda Navajo	Low	Plymouth Neon	NA
Mazda Protege	High	Plymouth Sundance	Average
Mazda RX-7	NA	Plymouth Voyager	Low
Mercedes-Benz C-class	NA	Pontiac Bonneville	Low
Mercedes-Benz E-class	Average	Pontiac Firebird	NA
Mercury Capri	High	Pontiac Grand Am	Average
Mercury Cougar	Average	Pontiac Grand Prix	Low
Mercury Grand Marquis	Low	Pontiac Sunbird	Average
Mercury Sable	Low	Pontiac Trans Sport	Low
Mercury Topaz	Average	Saab 900	NA
Mercury Tracer	Average	Saab 9000	Average
Mercury Villager	NA	Saturn	Average
Mitsubishi 3000 GT	High	Saturn SC	Average
Mitsubishi Diamante	Average	Subaru Impreza	NA
Mitsubishi Eclipse	High	Subaru Justy	High
Mitsubishi Expo LRV	Average		

CAR NAME	INSURANCE	CAR NAME	INSURANCE
Subaru Legacy	Average	Toyota Paseo	High
Subaru Loyale Wagon	NA	Toyota Previa	Average
Subaru SVX	Average	Toyota Supra	NA
Suzuki Sidekick	High	Toyota Tercel	High
Suzuki Swift	High	Volkswagen Corrado	High
Toyota 4Runner	High	Volkswagen EuroVan	NA
Toyota Camry	Low	Volkswagen Golf III	NA
Toyota Celica	NA	Volkswagen Jetta III	NA
Toyota Corolla	Average	Volkswagen Passat	Average
Toyota Land Cruiser	Average	Volvo 850GLT	NA
Toyota MR2	NA	Volvo 940/960	Low

Glossary of Auto Insurance Terms

—

Actual cash value. The amount of money received from the insurer for property that has been stolen or destroyed. Also, replacement cost minus depreciation.

Actuary. A professional trained in insurance risks who calculates insurance rates, appropriate reserves, and other aspects of the business.

Adjuster. Someone who investigates claims, determines their value, and attempts to settle them.

Agent. A person licensed by a state to sell and service insurance policies. An *independent agent* works for him- or herself, but represents two or more companies on a commission basis. An *exclusive agent* represents only one company, also on a commission basis.

Arbitration. When impartial experts determine the value or extent of damage or resolve disputes involving coverage and liability. One type of arbitration is *binding,* meaning that the decision of the experts is final and must be followed by the disputing parties.

Assigned-risk plan. A state-sponsored system that insures motorists who can't get coverage from private insurers. Also known as a high-risk or shared-risk plan.

Automobile physical damage insurance. Insurance covering a car and sometimes the property in it. Includes collision and comprehensive coverage.

Bodily injury liability insurance. Coverage bought by drivers to protect anyone they injure in an auto accident. The coverage pays medical costs incurred from bodily injury, sickness, or death related to the accident, as well as legal fees and damages involved in pain-and-suffering lawsuits arising from the accident.

Broker. A licensed, independent businessperson who represents a driver in finding insurance. Brokers are paid a commission by the companies with which they do business.

Claim. A request for payment from an

insurer when a driver has sustained a loss in an accident, whether for bodily injury, property damage, or both.

CLUE. Comprehensive Loss Underwriting Exchange: A data base owned by Equifax Inc., which includes auto insurance claims information on individuals. The information is submitted by insurers.

Collision insurance. Protection against damage to a car in the event it collides with another car or object, or rolls over.

Comprehensive auto insurance. Protection against damage to a car, but not related to a collision. This insurance covers theft and damage from fire, wind, flood, and vandalism, among other events.

Conditions. A driver's and insurer's rights and obligations as stated in the insurance contract.

Contributory negligence. The carelessness of an insured person, who may have been partially to blame for an accident.

Declarations. The portion of the insurance policy describing duration, types, limits, and prices of coverages, as well as the names of all persons and cars insured.

Deductible. A predetermined dollar figure that is the policyholder's share of costs arising from a particular claim or accident. The policyholder chooses the amount of the deductible, and must pay it out-of-pocket before the insurer pays its share.

Direct writer. An insurer that uses sales and service employees—not independent agents. Many direct writers deal with consumers by telephone or mail.

Disability threshold. In no-fault states (see page 60) with this provision, drivers cannot sue for pain-and-suffering damages unless they have been disabled by an accident for a specific period of time. The definition of that period and the required severity of the disability differ from state to state.

Dollar threshold. In no-fault states with this provision, drivers cannot sue for pain-and-suffering damages until their medical costs exceed a dollar value. That value varies from state to state. Also known as a *monetary threshold.*

Exclusion. A clause in the insurance policy that specifies situations, people, places, and property that the insurance doesn't cover.

Financial responsibility law. A statute that requires drivers to prove to the state they have the means to cover accident damages, at least up to the minimum required state liability limits. In most states, the law must be met by purchasing auto insurance.

High-risk plan. Also called shared-risk or assigned-risk plan. A state-sponsored system for insuring the cars of drivers who can't get coverage from private insurers. High-risk plans take many forms, including assigned-risk plans, joint underwriting associations, and reinsurance facilities.

Indemnity. Reimbursement for a loss.

Insured. Any person covered by an insurance policy.

Joint underwriting association (JUA). A state-sponsored high-risk plan to make auto insurance available to drivers who can't get coverage from private insurers.

Limit. The highest dollar amount a policy will pay for a particular coverage.

Medical payments auto insurance. An optional coverage that pays drivers' (and their family members') medical and funeral expenses arising from an automobile accident.

Mutual company. An insurance company owned by the policyholders.

Negligence. The failure of a person to act with the degree of care expected of a reasonably prudent person under similar circumstances.

No-fault automobile insurance. A type of coverage in which a driver's medical bills and other financial losses resulting from an automobile accident are reimbursed by his or her own insurance company, regardless of who was at fault.

Pay-at-the-pump. An auto insurance system, not yet practiced in the United States, under which drivers would buy automobile liability coverage through per-gallon gasoline charges, rather than through premiums paid directly to an insurance company.

Personal-injury protection (PIP). In no-fault states, medical coverage for the buyer of the insurance policy, and anyone else covered by the policy. Depending on state laws, PIP can also include coverage for loss of income, essential services, and other expenses.

Policy. A contract for insurance coverage.

Policyholder. A person who pays a premium to an insurer in return for expected protection. The policyholder "owns" the policy.

Premium. The amount paid to buy insurance coverage.

Rate. The basic charge or price upon which an individual's premium is based.

Rating territory. A geographical region in which the residents are theoretically grouped together for the establishment of an insurance rating system. Rating territories often differ from one another in traffic density, theft and accident rates, and other factors that affect insurance pricing.

Residual market. That portion of the population that is unable to buy insurance from private companies. The residual auto insurance market must resort to state-sponsored high-risk plans for its coverage.

Risk. Chance or likelihood of loss. Insurers also refer to the insured person as a "risk."

Shared-risk plan. *See* High-risk plan.

Stock company. A type of insurance company owned by shareholders or stockholders.

Subrogation. The process by which one insurer, having paid its policyholder for a loss, attempts to get reimbursed by another insurer or person who is legally liable for the loss.

Tort. A wrongful act that can be used as the basis of a civil lawsuit, such as a suit for pain and suffering.

Umbrella coverage. Insurance protection in excess of one's other liability insurance coverages. Umbrella coverage often includes protection of an individual's home and auto, and may include certain situations (such as libel) that are not covered by other policies.

Underinsured motorist coverage. Medical insurance for drivers and their passengers that is activated if they are struck by a motorist with insufficient medical liability insurance to cover the costs of their injuries.

Underwriting. The process by which an insurer decides which drivers to insure, which coverage to offer them, and how much to charge based on the drivers' characteristics and experience.

Uninsured motorist coverage. Medical insurance for drivers and their passengers that is activated if they are struck by another driver with no liability coverage. It also covers drivers and passengers if they are struck by a hit-and-run driver.

Verbal threshold. In no-fault states, a verbal description of the types and degrees of injuries for which a person injured in an auto accident may sue another for pain and suffering.

Voluntary market. The "regular," private insurance market in which motorists obtain coverage without state help.

Index

—